ISBN 0-8373-2146-8

C-2146   CAREER EXAMINATION SERIES

This is your
PASSBOOK® for...

Labor Specialist

Test Preparation Study Guide

Questions & Answers

NLC

NATIONAL LEARNING CORPORATION

PASSBOOK®

NOTICE

PASSBOOK® SERIES

THE *PASSBOOK® SERIES* has been created to prepare applicants and candidates for the ultimate academic battlefield – the examination room.

At some time in our lives, each and every one of us may be required to take an examination – for validation, matriculation, admission, qualification, registration, certification, or licensure.

Based on the assumption that every applicant or candidate has met the basic formal educational standards, has taken the required number of courses, and read the necessary texts, the *PASSBOOK® SERIES* furnishes the one special preparation which may assure passing with confidence, instead of failing with insecurity. Examination questions – together with answers – are furnished as the basic vehicle for study so that the mysteries of the examination and its compounding difficulties may be eliminated or diminished by a sure method.

This book is meant to help you pass your examination provided that you qualify and are serious in your objective.

The entire field is reviewed through the huge store of content information which is succinctly presented through a provocative and challenging approach – the question-and-answer method.

A climate of success is established by furnishing the correct answers at the end of each test.

You soon learn to recognize types of questions, forms of questions, and patterns of questioning. You may even begin to anticipate expected outcomes.

You perceive that many questions are repeated or adapted so that you can gain acute insights, which may enable you to score many sure points.

You learn how to confront new questions, or types of questions, and to attack them confidently and work out the correct answers.

You note objectives and emphases, and recognize pitfalls and dangers, so that you may make positive educational adjustments.

Moreover, you are kept fully informed in relation to new concepts, methods, practices, and directions in the field.

You discover that you are actually taking the examination all the time: you are preparing for the examination by "taking" an examination, not by reading extraneous and/or supererogatory textbooks.

In short, this PASSBOOK®, used directedly, should be an important factor in helping you to pass your test.

LABOR SPECIALIST

DUTIES
Supervises the field activities of Labor Technicians or participants of employment and training, or field work programs to ensure that participants and work site supervisors are aware of the principles, objectives and operating procedures of the programs. Evaluates the effectiveness of work/training experience and reviews complaints as they occur. Assists applicants in analyzing and evaluating their aptitude, interests, experience and training in terms of available positions. Develops employability plans, identifies bars to employment and recommends actions required to remove them. Performs related work as required.

SCOPE OF THE EXAMINATION
The written test will cover knowledge, skills, and/or abilities in such areas as:
1. Labor market, poverty, and unemployment concepts related to employment and training programs;
2. Collection, interpretation and utilization of data;
3. Understanding and interpreting written material;
4. Interviewing; and
5. Preparing written material.

HOW TO TAKE A TEST

I. YOU MUST PASS AN EXAMINATION

A. WHAT EVERY CANDIDATE SHOULD KNOW

Examination applicants often ask us for help in preparing for the written test. What can I study in advance? What kinds of questions will be asked? How will the test be given? How will the papers be graded?

As an applicant for a civil service examination, you may be wondering about some of these things. Our purpose here is to suggest effective methods of advance study and to describe civil service examinations.

Your chances for success on this examination can be increased if you know how to prepare. Those "pre-examination jitters" can be reduced if you know what to expect. You can even experience an adventure in good citizenship if you know why civil service exams are given.

B. WHY ARE CIVIL SERVICE EXAMINATIONS GIVEN?

Civil service examinations are important to you in two ways. As a citizen, you want public jobs filled by employees who know how to do their work. As a job seeker, you want a fair chance to compete for that job on an equal footing with other candidates. The best-known means of accomplishing this two-fold goal is the competitive examination.

Exams are widely publicized throughout the nation. They may be administered for jobs in federal, state, city, municipal, town or village governments or agencies.

Any citizen may apply, with some limitations, such as the age or residence of applicants. Your experience and education may be reviewed to see whether you meet the requirements for the particular examination. When these requirements exist, they are reasonable and applied consistently to all applicants. Thus, a competitive examination may cause you some uneasiness now, but it is your privilege and safeguard.

C. HOW ARE CIVIL SERVICE EXAMS DEVELOPED?

Examinations are carefully written by trained technicians who are specialists in the field known as "psychological measurement," in consultation with recognized authorities in the field of work that the test will cover. These experts recommend the subject matter areas or skills to be tested; only those knowledges or skills important to your success on the job are included. The most reliable books and source materials available are used as references. Together, the experts and technicians judge the difficulty level of the questions.

Test technicians know how to phrase questions so that the problem is clearly stated. Their ethics do not permit "trick" or "catch" questions. Questions may have been tried out on sample groups, or subjected to statistical analysis, to determine their usefulness.

Written tests are often used in combination with performance tests, ratings of training and experience, and oral interviews. All of these measures combine to form the best-known means of finding the right person for the right job.

II. HOW TO PASS THE WRITTEN TEST

A. NATURE OF THE EXAMINATION

To prepare intelligently for civil service examinations, you should know how they differ from school examinations you have taken. In school you were assigned certain definite pages to read or subjects to cover. The examination questions were quite detailed and usually emphasized memory. Civil service exams, on the other hand, try to discover your present ability to perform the duties of a position, plus your potentiality to learn these duties. In other words, a civil service exam attempts to predict how successful you will be. Questions cover such a broad area that they cannot be as minute and detailed as school exam questions.

In the public service similar kinds of work, or positions, are grouped together in one "class." This process is known as *position-classification*. All the positions in a class are paid according to the salary range for that class. One class title covers all of these positions, and they are all tested by the same examination.

B. FOUR BASIC STEPS

1) Study the announcement

How, then, can you know what subjects to study? Our best answer is: "Learn as much as possible about the class of positions for which you've applied." The exam will test the knowledge, skills and abilities needed to do the work.

Your most valuable source of information about the position you want is the official exam announcement. This announcement lists the training and experience qualifications. Check these standards and apply only if you come reasonably close to meeting them.

The brief description of the position in the examination announcement offers some clues to the subjects which will be tested. Think about the job itself. Review the duties in your mind. Can you perform them, or are there some in which you are rusty? Fill in the blank spots in your preparation.

Many jurisdictions preview the written test in the exam announcement by including a section called "Knowledge and Abilities Required," "Scope of the Examination," or some similar heading. Here you will find out specifically what fields will be tested.

2) Review your own background

Once you learn in general what the position is all about, and what you need to know to do the work, ask yourself which subjects you already know fairly well and which need improvement. You may wonder whether to concentrate on improving your strong areas or on building some background in your fields of weakness. When the announcement has specified "some knowledge" or "considerable knowledge," or has used adjectives like "beginning principles of..." or "advanced ... methods," you can get a clue as to the number and difficulty of questions to be asked in any given field. More questions, and hence broader coverage, would be included for those subjects which are more important in the work. Now weigh your strengths and weaknesses against the job requirements and prepare accordingly.

3) Determine the level of the position

Another way to tell how intensively you should prepare is to understand the level of the job for which you are applying. Is it the entering level? In other words, is this the position in which beginners in a field of work are hired? Or is it an intermediate or advanced level? Sometimes this is indicated by such words as "Junior" or "Senior" in the class title. Other jurisdictions use Roman numerals to designate the level – Clerk I, Clerk II, for example. The word "Supervisor" sometimes appears in the title. If the level is not indicated by the title, check the description of duties. Will you be working under very close supervision, or will you have responsibility for independent decisions in this work?

4) Choose appropriate study materials

Now that you know the subjects to be examined and the relative amount of each subject to be covered, you can choose suitable study materials. For beginning level jobs, or even advanced ones, if you have a pronounced weakness in some aspect of your training, read a modern, standard textbook in that field. Be sure it is up to date and has general coverage. Such books are normally available at your library, and the librarian will be glad to help you locate one. For entry-level positions, questions of appropriate difficulty are chosen – neither highly advanced questions, nor those too simple. Such questions require careful thought but not advanced training.

If the position for which you are applying is technical or advanced, you will read more advanced, specialized material. If you are already familiar with the basic principles of your field, elementary textbooks would waste your time. Concentrate on advanced textbooks and technical periodicals. Think through the concepts and review difficult problems in your field.

These are all general sources. You can get more ideas on your own initiative, following these leads. For example, training manuals and publications of the government agency which employs workers in your field can be useful, particularly for technical and professional positions. A letter or visit to the government department involved may result in more specific study suggestions, and certainly will provide you with a more definite idea of the exact nature of the position you are seeking.

III. KINDS OF TESTS

Tests are used for purposes other than measuring knowledge and ability to perform specified duties. For some positions, it is equally important to test ability to make adjustments to new situations or to profit from training. In others, basic mental abilities not dependent on information are essential. Questions which test these things may not appear as pertinent to the duties of the position as those which test for knowledge and information. Yet they are often highly important parts of a fair examination. For very general questions, it is almost impossible to help you direct your study efforts. What we can do is to point out some of the more common of these general abilities needed in public service positions and describe some typical questions.

1) General information

Broad, general information has been found useful for predicting job success in some kinds of work. This is tested in a variety of ways, from vocabulary lists to questions about current events. Basic background in some field of work, such as sociology or economics, may be sampled in a group of questions. Often these are principles which have become familiar to most persons through exposure rather than through formal training. It is difficult to advise you how to study for these questions; being alert to the world around you is our best suggestion.

2) Verbal ability

An example of an ability needed in many positions is verbal or language ability. Verbal ability is, in brief, the ability to use and understand words. Vocabulary and grammar tests are typical measures of this ability. Reading comprehension or paragraph interpretation questions are common in many kinds of civil service tests. You are given a paragraph of written material and asked to find its central meaning.

3) Numerical ability

Number skills can be tested by the familiar arithmetic problem, by checking paired lists of numbers to see which are alike and which are different, or by interpreting charts and graphs. In the latter test, a graph may be printed in the test booklet which you are asked to use as the basis for answering questions.

4) Observation

A popular test for law-enforcement positions is the observation test. A picture is shown to you for several minutes, then taken away. Questions about the picture test your ability to observe both details and larger elements.

5) Following directions

In many positions in the public service, the employee must be able to carry out written instructions dependably and accurately. You may be given a chart with several columns, each column listing a variety of information. The questions require you to carry out directions involving the information given in the chart.

6) Skills and aptitudes

Performance tests effectively measure some manual skills and aptitudes. When the skill is one in which you are trained, such as typing or shorthand, you can practice. These tests are often very much like those given in business school or high school courses. For many of the other skills and aptitudes, however, no short-time preparation can be made. Skills and abilities natural to you or that you have developed throughout your lifetime are being tested.

Many of the general questions just described provide all the data needed to answer the questions and ask you to use your reasoning ability to find the answers. Your best preparation for these tests, as well as for tests of facts and ideas, is to be at your physical and mental best. You, no doubt, have your own methods of getting into an exam-taking mood and keeping "in shape." The next section lists some ideas on this subject.

IV. KINDS OF QUESTIONS

Only rarely is the "essay" question, which you answer in narrative form, used in civil service tests. Civil service tests are usually of the short-answer type. Full instructions for answering these questions will be given to you at the examination. But in case this is your first experience with short-answer questions and separate answer sheets, here is what you need to know:

1) Multiple-choice Questions

Most popular of the short-answer questions is the "multiple choice" or "best answer" question. It can be used, for example, to test for factual knowledge, ability to solve problems or judgment in meeting situations found at work.

A multiple-choice question is normally one of three types—

- It can begin with an incomplete statement followed by several possible endings. You are to find the one ending which *best* completes the statement, although some of the others may not be entirely wrong.
- It can also be a complete statement in the form of a question which is answered by choosing one of the statements listed.

- It can be in the form of a problem – again you select the best answer.

Here is an example of a multiple-choice question with a discussion which should give you some clues as to the method for choosing the right answer:

When an employee has a complaint about his assignment, the action which will *best* help him overcome his difficulty is to
- A. discuss his difficulty with his coworkers
- B. take the problem to the head of the organization
- C. take the problem to the person who gave him the assignment
- D. say nothing to anyone about his complaint

In answering this question, you should study each of the choices to find which is best. Consider choice "A" – Certainly an employee may discuss his complaint with fellow employees, but no change or improvement can result, and the complaint remains unresolved. Choice "B" is a poor choice since the head of the organization probably does not know what assignment you have been given, and taking your problem to him is known as "going over the head" of the supervisor. The supervisor, or person who made the assignment, is the person who can clarify it or correct any injustice. Choice "C" is, therefore, correct. To say nothing, as in choice "D," is unwise. Supervisors have and interest in knowing the problems employees are facing, and the employee is seeking a solution to his problem.

2) True/False Questions

The "true/false" or "right/wrong" form of question is sometimes used. Here a complete statement is given. Your job is to decide whether the statement is right or wrong.

SAMPLE: A roaming cell-phone call to a nearby city costs less than a non-roaming call to a distant city.

This statement is wrong, or false, since roaming calls are more expensive.

This is not a complete list of all possible question forms, although most of the others are variations of these common types. You will always get complete directions for answering questions. Be sure you understand *how* to mark your answers – ask questions until you do.

V. RECORDING YOUR ANSWERS

Computer terminals are used more and more today for many different kinds of exams.

For an examination with very few applicants, you may be told to record your answers in the test booklet itself. Separate answer sheets are much more common. If this separate answer sheet is to be scored by machine – and this is often the case – it is highly important that you mark your answers correctly in order to get credit.

An electronic scoring machine is often used in civil service offices because of the speed with which papers can be scored. Machine-scored answer sheets must be marked with a pencil, which will be given to you. This pencil has a high graphite content which responds to the electronic scoring machine. As a matter of fact, stray dots may register as answers, so do not let your pencil rest on the answer sheet while you are pondering the correct answer. Also, if your pencil lead breaks or is otherwise defective, ask for another.

Since the answer sheet will be dropped in a slot in the scoring machine, be careful not to bend the corners or get the paper crumpled.

The answer sheet normally has five vertical columns of numbers, with 30 numbers to a column. These numbers correspond to the question numbers in your test booklet. After each number, going across the page are four or five pairs of dotted lines. These short dotted lines have small letters or numbers above them. The first two pairs may also have a "T" or "F" above the letters. This indicates that the first two pairs only are to be used if the questions are of the true-false type. If the questions are multiple choice, disregard the "T" and "F" and pay attention only to the small letters or numbers.

Answer your questions in the manner of the sample that follows:

32. The largest city in the United States is
    A. Washington, D.C.
    B. New York City
    C. Chicago
    D. Detroit
    E. San Francisco

1) Choose the answer you think is best. (New York City is the largest, so "B" is correct.)
2) Find the row of dotted lines numbered the same as the question you are answering. (Find row number 32)
3) Find the pair of dotted lines corresponding to the answer. (Find the pair of lines under the mark "B.")
4) Make a solid black mark between the dotted lines.

VI. BEFORE THE TEST

Common sense will help you find procedures to follow to get ready for an examination. Too many of us, however, overlook these sensible measures. Indeed, nervousness and fatigue have been found to be the most serious reasons why applicants fail to do their best on civil service tests. Here is a list of reminders:

- Begin your preparation early – Don't wait until the last minute to go scurrying around for books and materials or to find out what the position is all about.
- Prepare continuously – An hour a night for a week is better than an all-night cram session. This has been definitely established. What is more, a night a week for a month will return better dividends than crowding your study into a shorter period of time.
- Locate the place of the exam – You have been sent a notice telling you when and where to report for the examination. If the location is in a different town or otherwise unfamiliar to you, it would be well to inquire the best route and learn something about the building.
- Relax the night before the test – Allow your mind to rest. Do not study at all that night. Plan some mild recreation or diversion; then go to bed early and get a good night's sleep.
- Get up early enough to make a leisurely trip to the place for the test – This way unforeseen events, traffic snarls, unfamiliar buildings, etc. will not upset you.
- Dress comfortably – A written test is not a fashion show. You will be known by number and not by name, so wear something comfortable.

- Leave excess paraphernalia at home – Shopping bags and odd bundles will get in your way. You need bring only the items mentioned in the official notice you received; usually everything you need is provided. Do not bring reference books to the exam. They will only confuse those last minutes and be taken away from you when in the test room.
- Arrive somewhat ahead of time – If because of transportation schedules you must get there very early, bring a newspaper or magazine to take your mind off yourself while waiting.
- Locate the examination room – When you have found the proper room, you will be directed to the seat or part of the room where you will sit. Sometimes you are given a sheet of instructions to read while you are waiting. Do not fill out any forms until you are told to do so; just read them and be prepared.
- Relax and prepare to listen to the instructions
- If you have any physical problem that may keep you from doing your best, be sure to tell the test administrator. If you are sick or in poor health, you really cannot do your best on the exam. You can come back and take the test some other time.

VII. AT THE TEST

The day of the test is here and you have the test booklet in your hand. The temptation to get going is very strong. Caution! There is more to success than knowing the right answers. You must know how to identify your papers and understand variations in the type of short-answer question used in this particular examination. Follow these suggestions for maximum results from your efforts:

1) Cooperate with the monitor

The test administrator has a duty to create a situation in which you can be as much at ease as possible. He will give instructions, tell you when to begin, check to see that you are marking your answer sheet correctly, and so on. He is not there to guard you, although he will see that your competitors do not take unfair advantage. He wants to help you do your best.

2) Listen to all instructions

Don't jump the gun! Wait until you understand all directions. In most civil service tests you get more time than you need to answer the questions. So don't be in a hurry. Read each word of instructions until you clearly understand the meaning. Study the examples, listen to all announcements and follow directions. Ask questions if you do not understand what to do.

3) Identify your papers

Civil service exams are usually identified by number only. You will be assigned a number; you must not put your name on your test papers. Be sure to copy your number correctly. Since more than one exam may be given, copy your exact examination title.

4) Plan your time

Unless you are told that a test is a "speed" or "rate of work" test, speed itself is usually not important. Time enough to answer all the questions will be provided, but this does not mean that you have all day. An overall time limit has been set. Divide the total time (in minutes) by the number of questions to determine the approximate time you have for each question.

5) Do not linger over difficult questions

If you come across a difficult question, mark it with a paper clip (useful to have along) and come back to it when you have been through the booklet. One caution if you do this – be sure to skip a number on your answer sheet as well. Check often to be sure that you have not lost your place and that you are marking in the row numbered the same as the question you are answering.

6) Read the questions

Be sure you know what the question asks! Many capable people are unsuccessful because they failed to *read* the questions correctly.

7) Answer all questions

Unless you have been instructed that a penalty will be deducted for incorrect answers, it is better to guess than to omit a question.

8) Speed tests

It is often better NOT to guess on speed tests. It has been found that on timed tests people are tempted to spend the last few seconds before time is called in marking answers at random – without even reading them – in the hope of picking up a few extra points. To discourage this practice, the instructions may warn you that your score will be "corrected" for guessing. That is, a penalty will be applied. The incorrect answers will be deducted from the correct ones, or some other penalty formula will be used.

9) Review your answers

If you finish before time is called, go back to the questions you guessed or omitted to give them further thought. Review other answers if you have time.

10) Return your test materials

If you are ready to leave before others have finished or time is called, take ALL your materials to the monitor and leave quietly. Never take any test material with you. The monitor can discover whose papers are not complete, and taking a test booklet may be grounds for disqualification.

VIII. EXAMINATION TECHNIQUES

1) Read the general instructions carefully. These are usually printed on the first page of the exam booklet. As a rule, these instructions refer to the timing of the examination; the fact that you should not start work until the signal and must stop work at a signal, etc. If there are any *special* instructions, such as a choice of questions to be answered, make sure that you note this instruction carefully.

2) When you are ready to start work on the examination, that is as soon as the signal has been given, read the instructions to each question booklet, underline any key words or phrases, such as *least, best, outline, describe* and the like. In this way you will tend to answer as requested rather than discover on reviewing your paper that you *listed without describing*, that you selected the *worst* choice rather than the *best* choice, etc.

3) If the examination is of the objective or multiple-choice type – that is, each question will also give a series of possible answers: A, B, C or D, and you are called upon to select the best answer and write the letter next to that answer on your answer paper – it is advisable to start answering each question in turn. There may be anywhere from 50 to 100 such questions in the three or four hours allotted and you can see how much time would be taken if you read through all the questions before beginning to answer any. Furthermore, if you come across a question or group of questions which you know would be difficult to answer, it would undoubtedly affect your handling of all the other questions.

4) If the examination is of the essay type and contains but a few questions, it is a moot point as to whether you should read all the questions before starting to answer any one. Of course, if you are given a choice – say five out of seven and the like – then it is essential to read all the questions so you can eliminate the two that are most difficult. If, however, you are asked to answer all the questions, there may be danger in trying to answer the easiest one first because you may find that you will spend too much time on it. The best technique is to answer the first question, then proceed to the second, etc.

5) Time your answers. Before the exam begins, write down the time it started, then add the time allowed for the examination and write down the time it must be completed, then divide the time available somewhat as follows:
   - If 3-1/2 hours are allowed, that would be 210 minutes. If you have 80 objective-type questions, that would be an average of 2-1/2 minutes per question. Allow yourself no more than 2 minutes per question, or a total of 160 minutes, which will permit about 50 minutes to review.
   - If for the time allotment of 210 minutes there are 7 essay questions to answer, that would average about 30 minutes a question. Give yourself only 25 minutes per question so that you have about 35 minutes to review.

6) The most important instruction is to *read each question* and make sure you know what is wanted. The second most important instruction is to *time yourself properly* so that you answer every question. The third most important instruction is to *answer every question*. Guess if you have to but include something for each question. Remember that you will receive no credit for a blank and will probably receive some credit if you write something in answer to an essay question. If you guess a letter – say "B" for a multiple-choice question – you may have guessed right. If you leave a blank as an answer to a multiple-choice question, the examiners may respect your feelings but it will not add a point to your score. Some exams may penalize you for wrong answers, so in such cases *only*, you may not want to guess unless you have some basis for your answer.

7) Suggestions
   a. Objective-type questions
      1. Examine the question booklet for proper sequence of pages and questions
      2. Read all instructions carefully
      3. Skip any question which seems too difficult; return to it after all other questions have been answered
      4. Apportion your time properly; do not spend too much time on any single question or group of questions

5. Note and underline key words – *all, most, fewest, least, best, worst, same, opposite*, etc.
6. Pay particular attention to negatives
7. Note unusual option, e.g., unduly long, short, complex, different or similar in content to the body of the question
8. Observe the use of "hedging" words – *probably, may, most likely*, etc.
9. Make sure that your answer is put next to the same number as the question
10. Do not second-guess unless you have good reason to believe the second answer is definitely more correct
11. Cross out original answer if you decide another answer is more accurate; do not erase until you are ready to hand your paper in
12. Answer all questions; guess unless instructed otherwise
13. Leave time for review

b. Essay questions
1. Read each question carefully
2. Determine exactly what is wanted. Underline key words or phrases.
3. Decide on outline or paragraph answer
4. Include many different points and elements unless asked to develop any one or two points or elements
5. Show impartiality by giving pros and cons unless directed to select one side only
6. Make and write down any assumptions you find necessary to answer the questions
7. Watch your English, grammar, punctuation and choice of words
8. Time your answers; don't crowd material

8) Answering the essay question

Most essay questions can be answered by framing the specific response around several key words or ideas. Here are a few such key words or ideas:

M's: manpower, materials, methods, money, management
P's: purpose, program, policy, plan, procedure, practice, problems, pitfalls, personnel, public relations
  a. Six basic steps in handling problems:
    1. Preliminary plan and background development
    2. Collect information, data and facts
    3. Analyze and interpret information, data and facts
    4. Analyze and develop solutions as well as make recommendations
    5. Prepare report and sell recommendations
    6. Install recommendations and follow up effectiveness

  b. Pitfalls to avoid
    1. *Taking things for granted* – A statement of the situation does not necessarily imply that each of the elements is necessarily true; for example, a complaint may be invalid and biased so that all that can be taken for granted is that a complaint has been registered

2. *Considering only one side of a situation* – Wherever possible, indicate several alternatives and then point out the reasons you selected the best one
3. *Failing to indicate follow up* – Whenever your answer indicates action on your part, make certain that you will take proper follow-up action to see how successful your recommendations, procedures or actions turn out to be
4. *Taking too long in answering any single question* – Remember to time your answers properly

IX. AFTER THE TEST

Scoring procedures differ in detail among civil service jurisdictions although the general principles are the same. Whether the papers are hand-scored or graded by machine we have described, they are nearly always graded by number. That is, the person who marks the paper knows only the number – never the name – of the applicant. Not until all the papers have been graded will they be matched with names. If other tests, such as training and experience or oral interview ratings have been given, scores will be combined. Different parts of the examination usually have different weights. For example, the written test might count 60 percent of the final grade, and a rating of training and experience 40 percent. In many jurisdictions, veterans will have a certain number of points added to their grades.

After the final grade has been determined, the names are placed in grade order and an eligible list is established. There are various methods for resolving ties between those who get the same final grade – probably the most common is to place first the name of the person whose application was received first. Job offers are made from the eligible list in the order the names appear on it. You will be notified of your grade and your rank as soon as all these computations have been made. This will be done as rapidly as possible.

People who are found to meet the requirements in the announcement are called "eligibles." Their names are put on a list of eligible candidates. An eligible's chances of getting a job depend on how high he stands on this list and how fast agencies are filling jobs from the list.

When a job is to be filled from a list of eligibles, the agency asks for the names of people on the list of eligibles for that job. When the civil service commission receives this request, it sends to the agency the names of the three people highest on this list. Or, if the job to be filled has specialized requirements, the office sends the agency the names of the top three persons who meet these requirements from the general list.

The appointing officer makes a choice from among the three people whose names were sent to him. If the selected person accepts the appointment, the names of the others are put back on the list to be considered for future openings.

That is the rule in hiring from all kinds of eligible lists, whether they are for typist, carpenter, chemist, or something else. For every vacancy, the appointing officer has his choice of any one of the top three eligibles on the list. This explains why the person whose name is on top of the list sometimes does not get an appointment when some of the persons lower on the list do. If the appointing officer chooses the second or third eligible, the No. 1 eligible does not get a job at once, but stays on the list until he is appointed or the list is terminated.

X. HOW TO PASS THE INTERVIEW TEST

The examination for which you applied requires an oral interview test. You have already taken the written test and you are now being called for the interview test – the final part of the formal examination.

You may think that it is not possible to prepare for an interview test and that there are no procedures to follow during an interview. Our purpose is to point out some things you can do in advance that will help you and some good rules to follow and pitfalls to avoid while you are being interviewed.

What is an interview supposed to test?

The written examination is designed to test the technical knowledge and competence of the candidate; the oral is designed to evaluate intangible qualities, not readily measured otherwise, and to establish a list showing the relative fitness of each candidate – as measured against his competitors – for the position sought. Scoring is not on the basis of "right" and "wrong," but on a sliding scale of values ranging from "not passable" to "outstanding." As a matter of fact, it is possible to achieve a relatively low score without a single "incorrect" answer because of evident weakness in the qualities being measured.

Occasionally, an examination may consist entirely of an oral test – either an individual or a group oral. In such cases, information is sought concerning the technical knowledges and abilities of the candidate, since there has been no written examination for this purpose. More commonly, however, an oral test is used to supplement a written examination.

Who conducts interviews?

The composition of oral boards varies among different jurisdictions. In nearly all, a representative of the personnel department serves as chairman. One of the members of the board may be a representative of the department in which the candidate would work. In some cases, "outside experts" are used, and, frequently, a businessman or some other representative of the general public is asked to serve. Labor and management or other special groups may be represented. The aim is to secure the services of experts in the appropriate field.

However the board is composed, it is a good idea (and not at all improper or unethical) to ascertain in advance of the interview who the members are and what groups they represent. When you are introduced to them, you will have some idea of their backgrounds and interests, and at least you will not stutter and stammer over their names.

What should be done before the interview?

While knowledge about the board members is useful and takes some of the surprise element out of the interview, there is other preparation which is more substantive. It *is* possible to prepare for an oral interview – in several ways:

1) Keep a copy of your application and review it carefully before the interview

This may be the only document before the oral board, and the starting point of the interview. Know what education and experience you have listed there, and the sequence and dates of all of it. Sometimes the board will ask you to review the highlights of your experience for them; you should not have to hem and haw doing it.

2) Study the class specification and the examination announcement

Usually, the oral board has one or both of these to guide them. The qualities, characteristics or knowledges required by the position sought are stated in these documents. They offer valuable clues as to the nature of the oral interview. For example, if the job involves supervisory responsibilities, the announcement will usually indicate that knowledge of modern supervisory methods and the qualifications of the candidate as a supervisor will be tested. If so, you can expect such questions, frequently in the form of a hypothetical situation which you are expected to solve. NEVER go into an oral without knowledge of the duties and responsibilities of the job you seek.

3) Think through each qualification required

Try to visualize the kind of questions you would ask if you were a board member. How well could you answer them? Try especially to appraise your own knowledge and background in each area, *measured against the job sought*, and identify any areas in which you are weak. Be critical and realistic – do not flatter yourself.

4) Do some general reading in areas in which you feel you may be weak

For example, if the job involves supervision and your past experience has NOT, some general reading in supervisory methods and practices, particularly in the field of human relations, might be useful. Do NOT study agency procedures or detailed manuals. The oral board will be testing your understanding and capacity, not your memory.

5) Get a good night's sleep and watch your general health and mental attitude

You will want a clear head at the interview. Take care of a cold or any other minor ailment, and of course, no hangovers.

What should be done on the day of the interview?

Now comes the day of the interview itself. Give yourself plenty of time to get there. Plan to arrive somewhat ahead of the scheduled time, particularly if your appointment is in the fore part of the day. If a previous candidate fails to appear, the board might be ready for you a bit early. By early afternoon an oral board is almost invariably behind schedule if there are many candidates, and you may have to wait. Take along a book or magazine to read, or your application to review, but leave any extraneous material in the waiting room when you go in for your interview. In any event, relax and compose yourself.

The matter of dress is important. The board is forming impressions about you – from your experience, your manners, your attitude, and your appearance. Give your personal appearance careful attention. Dress your best, but not your flashiest. Choose conservative, appropriate clothing, and be sure it is immaculate. This is a business interview, and your appearance should indicate that you regard it as such. Besides, being well groomed and properly dressed will help boost your confidence.

Sooner or later, someone will call your name and escort you into the interview room. *This is it.* From here on you are on your own. It is too late for any more preparation. But remember, you asked for this opportunity to prove your fitness, and you are here because your request was granted.

What happens when you go in?

The usual sequence of events will be as follows: The clerk (who is often the board stenographer) will introduce you to the chairman of the oral board, who will introduce you to the other members of the board. Acknowledge the introductions before you sit down. Do not be surprised if you find a microphone facing you or a stenotypist sitting by. Oral interviews are usually recorded in the event of an appeal or other review.

Usually the chairman of the board will open the interview by reviewing the highlights of your education and work experience from your application – primarily for the benefit of the other members of the board, as well as to get the material into the record. Do not interrupt or comment unless there is an error or significant misinterpretation; if that is the case, do not hesitate. But do not quibble about insignificant matters. Also, he will usually ask you some question about your education, experience or your present job – partly to get you to start talking and to establish the interviewing "rapport." He may start the actual questioning, or turn it over to one of the other members. Frequently, each member undertakes the questioning on a particular area, one in which he is perhaps most competent, so you can expect each member to participate in the examination. Because time is limited, you may also expect some rather abrupt switches in the direction the questioning takes, so do not be upset by it. Normally, a board member will not pursue a single line of questioning unless he discovers a particular strength or weakness.

After each member has participated, the chairman will usually ask whether any member has any further questions, then will ask you if you have anything you wish to add. Unless you are expecting this question, it may floor you. Worse, it may start you off on an extended, extemporaneous speech. The board is not usually seeking more information. The question is principally to offer you a last opportunity to present further qualifications or to indicate that you have nothing to add. So, if you feel that a significant qualification or characteristic has been overlooked, it is proper to point it out in a sentence or so. Do not compliment the board on the thoroughness of their examination – they have been sketchy, and you know it. If you wish, merely say, "No thank you, I have nothing further to add." This is a point where you can "talk yourself out" of a good impression or fail to present an important bit of information. Remember, *you close the interview yourself.*

The chairman will then say, "That is all, Mr. _____, thank you." Do not be startled; the interview is over, and quicker than you think. Thank him, gather your belongings and take your leave. Save your sigh of relief for the other side of the door.

How to put your best foot forward

Throughout this entire process, you may feel that the board individually and collectively is trying to pierce your defenses, seek out your hidden weaknesses and embarrass and confuse you. Actually, this is not true. They are obliged to make an appraisal of your qualifications for the job you are seeking, and they want to see you in your best light. Remember, they must interview all candidates and a non-cooperative candidate may become a failure in spite of their best efforts to bring out his qualifications. Here are 15 suggestions that will help you:

1) Be natural – Keep your attitude confident, not cocky

If you are not confident that you can do the job, do not expect the board to be. Do not apologize for your weaknesses, try to bring out your strong points. The board is interested in a positive, not negative, presentation. Cockiness will antagonize any board member and make him wonder if you are covering up a weakness by a false show of strength.

2) Get comfortable, but don't lounge or sprawl

Sit erectly but not stiffly. A careless posture may lead the board to conclude that you are careless in other things, or at least that you are not impressed by the importance of the occasion. Either conclusion is natural, even if incorrect. Do not fuss with your clothing, a pencil or an ashtray. Your hands may occasionally be useful to emphasize a point; do not let them become a point of distraction.

3) Do not wisecrack or make small talk

This is a serious situation, and your attitude should show that you consider it as such. Further, the time of the board is limited – they do not want to waste it, and neither should you.

4) Do not exaggerate your experience or abilities

In the first place, from information in the application or other interviews and sources, the board may know more about you than you think. Secondly, you probably will not get away with it. An experienced board is rather adept at spotting such a situation, so do not take the chance.

5) If you know a board member, do not make a point of it, yet do not hide it

Certainly you are not fooling him, and probably not the other members of the board. Do not try to take advantage of your acquaintanceship – it will probably do you little good.

6) Do not dominate the interview

Let the board do that. They will give you the clues – do not assume that you have to do all the talking. Realize that the board has a number of questions to ask you, and do not try to take up all the interview time by showing off your extensive knowledge of the answer to the first one.

7) Be attentive

You only have 20 minutes or so, and you should keep your attention at its sharpest throughout. When a member is addressing a problem or question to you, give him your undivided attention. Address your reply principally to him, but do not exclude the other board members.

8) Do not interrupt

A board member may be stating a problem for you to analyze. He will ask you a question when the time comes. Let him state the problem, and wait for the question.

9) Make sure you understand the question

Do not try to answer until you are sure what the question is. If it is not clear, restate it in your own words or ask the board member to clarify it for you. However, do not haggle about minor elements.

10) Reply promptly but not hastily

A common entry on oral board rating sheets is "candidate responded readily," or "candidate hesitated in replies." Respond as promptly and quickly as you can, but do not jump to a hasty, ill-considered answer.

11) Do not be peremptory in your answers

A brief answer is proper – but do not fire your answer back. That is a losing game from your point of view. The board member can probably ask questions much faster than you can answer them.

12) Do not try to create the answer you think the board member wants

He is interested in what kind of mind you have and how it works – not in playing games. Furthermore, he can usually spot this practice and will actually grade you down on it.

13) Do not switch sides in your reply merely to agree with a board member

Frequently, a member will take a contrary position merely to draw you out and to see if you are willing and able to defend your point of view. Do not start a debate, yet do not surrender a good position. If a position is worth taking, it is worth defending.

14) Do not be afraid to admit an error in judgment if you are shown to be wrong

The board knows that you are forced to reply without any opportunity for careful consideration. Your answer may be demonstrably wrong. If so, admit it and get on with the interview.

15) Do not dwell at length on your present job

The opening question may relate to your present assignment. Answer the question but do not go into an extended discussion. You are being examined for a *new* job, not your present one. As a matter of fact, try to phrase ALL your answers in terms of the job for which you are being examined.

Basis of Rating

Probably you will forget most of these "do's" and "don'ts" when you walk into the oral interview room. Even remembering them all will not ensure you a passing grade. Perhaps you did not have the qualifications in the first place. But remembering them will help you to put your best foot forward, without treading on the toes of the board members.

Rumor and popular opinion to the contrary notwithstanding, an oral board wants you to make the best appearance possible. They know you are under pressure – but they also want to see how you respond to it as a guide to what your reaction would be under the pressures of the job you seek. They will be influenced by the degree of poise you display, the personal traits you show and the manner in which you respond.

ABOUT THIS BOOK

This book contains tests divided into Examination Sections. Go through each test, answering every question in the margin. We have also attached a sample answer sheet at the back of the book that can be removed and used. At the end of each test look at the answer key and check your answers. On the ones you got wrong, look at the right answer choice and learn. Do not fill in the answers first. Do not memorize the questions and answers, but understand the answer and principles involved. On your test, the questions will likely be different from the samples. Questions are changed and new ones added. If you understand these past questions you should have success with any changes that arise. Tests may consist of several types of questions. We have additional books on each subject should more study be advisable or necessary for you. Finally, the more you study, the better prepared you will be. This book is intended to be the last thing you study before you walk into the examination room. Prior study of relevant texts is also recommended. NLC publishes some of these in our Fundamental Series. Knowledge and good sense are important factors in passing your exam. Good luck also helps. So now study this Passbook, absorb the material contained within and take that knowledge into the examination. Then do your best to pass that exam.

———

EXAMINATION SECTION

EXAMINATION SECTION
TEST1

DIRECTIONS: Each question or incomplete statement is followed by several suggested answers or completions. Select the one that BEST answers the question or completes the statement. *PRINT THE LETTER OF THE CORRECT ANSWER IN THE SPACE AT THE RIGHT.*

1. According to most research, which of the following factors is generally considered by people as MOST important in deciding to take a job?

   A. Control of work schedule
   B. Salary/wage
   C. Effect on family or personal life
   D. Employer size

1.____

2. The first explicitly *pro-union* federal law passed in the United States was the

   A. Sherman Antitrust Act of 1890
   B. Clayton Act of 1914
   C. Norris-LaGuardia Act of 1932
   D. Wagner Act of 1935

2.____

3. _____ is the system condensing rate ranges into wider classifications for employee rating.

   A. Broadbanding   B. Codetermination
   C. Anchoring   D. Dilation

3.____

4. During an employment interview, which of the following items of information can be lawfully solicited from an applicant for the purpose of disqualification?

   A. Arrest record
   B. Prior marital status
   C. Military discharge status, if not the result of a military conviction
   D. Whether candidate has ever worked under a different name

4.____

5. Which of the following best describes the effect of the Industrial Revolution (late 18th century) on the field of human resources management?

   A. The proliferation of mid-level managers
   B. An increasing gap between workers and business owners
   C. A shorter workday for both management and labor
   D. More dangerous working conditions

5.____

6. The _____ shop is a practice in which management tries to avoid the organization of labor into a union, without violating labor laws.

   A. open   B. agency   C. restricted   D. preferential

6.____

7. In the field of human resources, the term *central tendency* refers to the

   A. inclination for all workers to perform at an average level
   B. most likely behavior from a group of employees in a given situation
   C. inclination for an employee to remain in a static state, with no desire for advancement
   D. rating of all or most of the employees in the middle of a performance scale

7.____

8. Of all the possible uses for performance evaluations within an organization, which tends to be most INFREQUENTLY used?   8._____

   A. Helping organization to identify individual employees' strengths and weaknesses
   B. Wage and salary administration
   C. Promoting communication between superiors and subordinates
   D. Performance feedback

9. The main obstacle that top management encounters in making strategic planning decisions regarding human resources is that   9._____

   A. workers increasingly demand to be included in the process
   B. all other resources are evaluated in terms of money, and in most organizations people are not
   C. human resources are not as important in capital-intensive organizations
   D. in some sectors, turnover rates are too high to allow accurate projections

10. In what year was the Occupational Safety and Health Administration (OSHA) formed?   10._____

   A. 1935   B. 1955   C. 1971   D. 1980

11. A(n) _____ test will measure how well an applicant can do a sample of work that is to be performed.   11._____

   A. proficiency   B. aptitude
   C. psychomotor   D. job knowledge

12. Which of the following groups is least likely to benefit from an organization's affirmative action program?   12._____

   A. Ethnic minorities   B. Religious minorities
   C. Women   D. Racial minorities

13. Which of the following statements about human resources management is LEAST supported by research and field experience?   13._____

   A. Human resources management should focus on quality, customer service, employee involvement, productivity, teamwork, and creating a flexible workforce.
   B. The biggest challenge for human resource managers is to shift their attention from current operations to developing strategies for the future.
   C. Human resource management practices and policies should be left to human resource managers, so that operating managers can focus on other elements of organizational success.
   D. Globalization, downsizing, and the changing demographics of the workforce are the external forces most likely to affect a company's competitiveness in the 21st century.

14. Each of the following is a commonly accepted function of the collective bargaining process, EXCEPT   14._____

    A. establishing a method for the settlement of disputes during the lifetime of a contract
    B. administering labor agreements
    C. determining the appropriate collective bargaining units among groups of workers
    D. establishing and revising the rules of the workplace

15. The degree to which a test, interview, or performance evaluation measures skills, knowledge, or an employee's ability to perform is known as _____ validity.   15._____

    A. criterion-related   B. construct
    C. skills   D. content

16. Which of the following items of legislation is designed to ensure that handicapped people are not refused a job merely because of their handicap if the handicap does not affect their ability to do a job?   16._____

    A. Civil Rights Act of 1964
    B. Rehabilitation Act
    C. Americans with Disabilities Act
    D. Civil Rights Act of 1991

17. Key or benchmark jobs used in pay surveys have each of the following characteristics EXCEPT   17._____

    A. they are free of discriminatory employment patterns
    B. they are subject to recent shortages or surpluses in the marketplace
    C. the work content is relatively stable over time
    D. a large number of employees hold them

18. In the human resource planning process, the first step taken is usually   18._____

    A. human resource supply analysis
    B. forecasting human resource demands
    C. action plan development
    D. situation analysis

19. In a typical workplace safety management program, the first step taken is typically to   19._____

    A. develop effective reporting systems
    B. reward supervisors for effective management of the safety function
    C. establish indicator systems such as accident statistics
    D. develop rules and procedures

20. Which of the following is NOT a power of the Equal Employment Opportunity Commission?   20._____
   To

   A. require employers to report employment statistics
   B. bring lawsuits against employers in the federal courts
   C. issue directly enforceable orders
   D. mediate an agreement between parties when a discrimination complaint is found justified

21. The most common job evaluation method used to determine pay structures within organizations is   21._____

   A. the point method   B. classification
   C. factor comparison   D. ranking

22. Which of the following items of federal legislation established a minimum wage for specified types of workers?   22._____

   A. Civil Rights Act of 1964
   B. Railway Labor Act
   C. Fair Labor Standards Act
   D. Occupational Health and Safety Act

23. Which of the following performance evaluation methods tends to be LEAST useful for the purpose of making promotion decisions?   23._____

   A. Behaviorally anchored rating system (BARS)
   B. Essay evaluations
   C. Critical incident
   D. Field review

24. During the planning process for a project, the phase occurs after the objective has been set, in which the supervisor must decide how the objective can be achieved, is typically referred to as the _____ phase.   24._____

   A. discussion   B. questioning
   C. action planning   D. preplanning

25. According to the EEC's definitions, sexual advances, requests for sexual favors, and other verbal or physical conduct of a sexual nature are considered sexual harassment under each of the following conditions EXCEPT   25._____

   A. submission to such conduct is, either explicitly or implicitly, a term or condition of a person's employment
   B. submission to or rejection of such conduct is used as the basis for employment decisions affecting the individual
   C. the advances or requests are unwelcome
   D. such conduct unreasonably interferes with an individual's work or creates a hostile or offensive work environment

KEY (CORRECT ANSWERS)

1.	C	11.	A
2.	C	12.	B
3.	A	13.	C
4.	D	14.	C
5.	B	15.	D
6.	C	16.	B
7.	D	17.	B
8.	C	18.	D
9.	B	19.	C
10.	C	20.	C

21.	A
22.	C
23.	B
24.	C
25.	C

———

TEST 2

DIRECTIONS: Each question or incomplete statement is followed by several suggested answers or completions. Select the one that BEST answers the question or completes the statement. *PRINT THE LETTER OF THE CORRECT ANSWER IN THE SPACE AT THE RIGHT.*

1. Which of the following conditions within an organization is LEAST favorable for implementing a gainsharing plan?

    A. Product costs are controllable by employees.
    B. The organization is fairly large, usually more than 500 employees.
    C. There is no labor union.
    D. There are few product changes.

1.____

2. The most widely used method for training employees is

    A. vestibule training
    B. computer-assisted instruction
    C. on-the-job training
    D. programmed instruction

2.____

3. In human resources management, the term *financial core* refers to

    A. the secure, low-return investments that stabilize an employee benefit plan
    B. the group of employees whose performance most directly impacts a company's earnings
    C. a company's primary product or service line
    D. members of a union who pay dues but choose not to engage in any other union-related activity

3.____

4. In the human resources planning process, which of the following activities is typically performed by the operating manager with input from the human resources manager?

    A. Analysis of personnel supply
    B. Strategic management decisions
    C. Forecasting personnel demands
    D. Job analysis

4.____

5. Title VII of the Civil Rights Act of 1964, as amended, prohibits discrimination based on race, color, religion, sex, or national origin in any term, condition, or privilege of employment. Each of the following types of organizations is subject to the provisions of this legislation EXCEPT

    A. all public and private educational institutions
    B. private employers of 15 or fewer people
    C. joint labor-management committees for apprenticeships and training
    D. all state and local governments

5.____

6. Job _____ is the term for a written explanation of the knowledge, skills, abilities, and other characteristics necessary for effective job performance.

    A. evaluation   B. specification
    C. description   D. analysis

6.____

7. In the performance evaluation process, which of the following functions is typically under-   7.____
    taken by the human resource manager and engineers, subject to the approval of an
    operating manager?

    A. Filing the performance evaluation
    B. Discussing the evaluation with the employee
    C. Establishing performance standards
    D. Reviewing employee performance

8. The purpose of a pay policy line is to   8.____

    A. summarize the pay rates of various jobs in the labor market
    B. represent an organization's pay level policy relative to what competition pays for
        similar jobs
    C. document compliance with the Equal Pay Act
    D. determine the minimum total payroll needed to maintain profit and productivity

9. Which of the following recruitment practices is least likely to be reviewed by a govern-   9.____
    ment agency for the purpose of determining possible discrimination?

    A. Estimates of the firm's employment needs for the coming year
    B. Statistics on the number of applicants processed by category
    C. Division of responsibilities between operating managers and human resource
        managers
    D. Recruiting advertising

10. Another name for *quality circles* in personnel is   10.____

    A. continuous improvement teams
    B. groupthink
    C. formal work groups
    D. functional departments

11. Before implementing an employee training program, an organization often conducts a   11.____
    needs assessment first. Which of the following techniques involves the greatest potential
    participant involvement in the process?

    A. Evaluation of past programs
    B. Attitude surveys
    C. Critical incident method
    D. Performance documents

12. In the vocabulary of job analysis, what is the term for a group of positions that are similar   12.____
    in their duties?

    A. Vocation   B. Task   C. Field   D. Job

13. When assessing the costs and benefits of their training and development programs, many firms rely on the consensus accounting model. According to this model, the final step in this process is

    A. determining all training cost categories
    B. coding training costs
    C. establishing an organization-specific definition of training
    D. calculating training costs

13.____

14. Equal _____ is NOT a factor used to define equal work under the terms of the Equal Pay Act.

    A. working conditions   B. effort
    C. training   D. skills

14.____

15. Typically, which of the following procedures in the employee selection process is conducted FIRST?

    A. Interview by human resources department
    B. Employment tests
    C. Interview by supervisor
    D. Background and reference checks

15.____

16. Which of the following is an individual performance assessment method?

    A. Forced distribution   B. Paired comparison
    C. Ranking   D. Forced choice

16.____

17. When a manager evaluates employees' performance by placing a certain percentage of personnel at various performance levels, the method of _____ is being used.

    A. forced-choice rating
    B. forced-distribution ranking
    C. alteration ranking
    D. central tendency

17.____

18. Though a *closed shop* organization is illegal under federal law, many modified closed shops still exist in U.S. labor. Which of the following industries is LEAST likely to operate such an organization?

    A. Maritime   B. Agriculture
    C. Printing   D. Construction

18.____

19. *Reliability* in personnel selection refers to how stable or repeatable a measurement is over a variety of testing conditions. Which of the following types of reliability is determined by correlating scores from two different configurations of the same selection test?

    A. Interrater   B. Alternate-form
    C. Criterion-related   D. Test-retest

19.____

20. In the overall union structure, intermediate union bodes are typically responsible for each   20.____
of the following EXCEPT

    A. collecting dues from individual members
    B. helping to coordinate union membership
    C. joining local unions with similar goals
    D. organizing discussion of issues pertaining to labor-management relationships

21. Historically, the big push in the United States for increasing employee benefits occurred   21.____
during____, when there was a shortage of work and wages were controlled by the federal government.

    A. the recession of 1890   B. the Great Depression
    C. World War II   D. the 1960s

22. An assessment center is a multiple-selection method for obtaining personnel. Which of   22.____
the following statements about assessment centers is generally FALSE?

    A. Assessors doing the evaluation are usually a panel of line managers from the orga-
nization.
    B. The centers are used mostly for selecting managers.
    C. The centers make extensive use of written tests as well as performance evalua-
tions.
    D. All evaluations of applicants are performed on an individual basis.

23. The first step in the collective bargaining process is typically   23.____

    A. fact-finding   B. conciliation
    C. negotiation   D. concession

24. To an employee, the MAIN advantage of a flexible spending account benefit is that   24.____

    A. different employees can be given different minimum spending levels, based on
their needs
    B. bills are paid with before-tax dollars
    C. they provide extensive major medical coverage
    D. money left in the account at the end of the year rolls over into the next

25. For which of the following purposes should performance evaluations be based on actual   25.____
performance rather than potential performance?
       I. Promotion consideration
     II. Salary and wage adjustment
   III. Improvement of performance
The CORRECT answer is

    A. I only   B. I, II   C. II, III   D. I, II, III

KEY (CORRECT ANSWERS)

1.	B	11.	C
2.	C	12.	D
3.	D	13.	B
4.	B	14.	C
5.	B	15.	A
6.	B	16.	D
7.	C	17.	B
8.	B	18.	B
9.	C	19.	B
10.	A	20.	A

21.	C
22.	D
23.	B
24.	B
25.	C

———

EXAMINATION SECTION
TEST 1

DIRECTIONS: Each question or incomplete statement is followed by several suggested answers or completions. Select the one that BEST answers the question or completes the statement. *PRINT THE LETTER OF THE CORRECT ANSWER IN THE SPACE AT THE RIGHT.*

1. Each of the following is currently a common reason for American employees to distrust unions EXCEPT

    A. the fact that some well-known union leaders have engaged in illegal acts
    B. the belief that unions stand against individualism and free enterprise
    C. they are viewed as an ineffective means of gaining contracts and processing complaints
    D. they are viewed as being dominated by blue-collar workers

1.____

2. The main disadvantage to using a structured interview approach during personnel selection is that it

    A. is usually more stressful for the interviewee
    B. can produce long periods of uncomfortable silence
    C. requires a good deal of training to conduct
    D. is usually very restrictive

2.____

3. Of the different strategies that may be implemented to control the costs of employee benefit plans, which of the following is LEAST likely to generate ill will on the part of employees?

    A. Increased co-payment or deductible
    B. Case management
    C. Preauthorization before covering certain expenses
    D. Requiring second opinions

3.____

4. In which of the following sectors is the National Mediation Board responsible for the final determination of appropriate collective bargaining units?

    A. Railway and airline   B. Postal
    C. Private   D. Federal

4.____

5. It is NOT a common reason for using a job evaluation plan to

    A. develop a basis for a merit pay program
    B. define expectations for individuals in specific jobs
    C. identify to employees a hierarchy of pay progression
    D. provide a basis for wage negotiation in collective bargaining

5.____

6. Which of the following is an example of a *content valid* test used in the personnel selection process?
A(n)

    A. written skills test for a short-order cook position
    B. unstructured interview for a supervisory position on a shop floor
    C. typing test for a secretarial position
    D. written personality assessment for a middle-management position at a consumer goods firm

6.____

7. Which of the following items of federal legislation specifies unfair labor union practices that are not permitted?

    A. Wagner Act
    B. Taft-Hartley Act
    C. Fair Labor Standards Act
    D. Landrum-Griffin Act

7.____

8. The MOST important drawback to implementing individual incentive systems is that they

    A. add pay increases to base pay
    B. limit the number of *important* tasks
    C. do not measure performance at the individual level
    D. often sabotage the interdependency of employees

8.____

9. During the labor organization process, if employees decide they no longer need a union, or when the union fails to negotiate an initial contract within the first _____ period of certification, decertification elections can be held.

    A. 90-day   B. 3-month   C. 6-month   D. 12-month

9.____

10. In the employee training programs of U.S. organizations, which of the following formal delivery methods is most likely to be used?

    A. Case studies
    B. Noncomputerized self-study
    C. Videotapes
    D. Role playing

10.____

11. In human resources management, the _____ principle states that a manager's authority must be equal to his or her responsibility.

    A. Peter   B. exception
    C. leadership   D. parity

11.____

12. Which of the following management approaches to collective bargaining illustrates the   12.____
tactic of *Boulwarism?*

    A. Responding to labor's offer by mirroring the negotiators' style, whether it is hard-
line or accommodating
    B. Viewing the opposition as an adversary, yet recognizing that an agreement must
be worked out along legal guidelines
    C. Presenting an initial offer as a final offer that will not be altered by negotiation
    D. Offering compromise, flexibility, and tolerance in order to bring negotiations to a
speedy conclusion

13. Which of the following is/are likely to be advantages associated with using job incum-   13.____
bents in the job analysis process?
      I. They are a better source of information about what work is actually being
done, rather than what is supposed to be done
     II. Increased acceptance of any work changes that might result from the analy-
sis
    III. They tend to have a clearer idea of the importance of their work than manag-
ers or supervisors
The CORRECT answer is

    A. I *only*   B. I, II   C. I, III   D. II, III

14. The risk of *negative recruitment* is generally highest when the method of _____ is used.   14.____

    A. summer internships
    B. job posting
    C. special-events recruiting
    D. college recruiting

15. Which of the following is NOT an element of merit pay?   15.____

    A. Increases based on individual performance evaluations
    B. Increases based on years of job-related experience
    C. Pay ranges designed to reflect differences in performance or experience
    D. Merit increase guidelines that translate a specific performance rating and position
in the pay range to a percent merit increase

16. In order to perform an unbiased performance evaluation, an evaluator keeps a diary of   16.____
employee performance. This practice will be most useful in avoiding the common
_____error in assessment.

    A. contrast effect   B. halo effect
    C. central tendency   D. recency of events

17. Which of the following is the most important factor in assessing claims of discrimination   17.____
    under the Civil Rights Act of 1991 and the Americans with Disabilities Act of 1990?
    The

    A.   company's overall work environment
    B.   diversity of the company's existing personnel
    C.   company's method for job analysis
    D.   size of the company

18. Employees are LEAST likely to accept performance appraisals involving rating by subor-   18.____
    dinates if the evaluations are used for the purpose of

    A.   determining raises or promotions
    B.   motivation
    C.   development
    D.   validation of selection tools

19. According to the achievement-power-affiliation theory, which of the following characteris-   19.____
    tics in an organization will have no effect on an employee's need for affiliation?

    A.   Responsibility   B.   Support
    C.   Conflict   D.   Reward

20. OSHA regulations state that each occupational injury and illness must be recorded on   20.____
    Form 200 within _____ from the time the employer first learned of the injury or illness.

    A.   48 hours   B.   6 working days
    C.   10 days   D.   30 days

21. _____ authority is used to support and advise line authority.   21.____

    A.   Unstructured   B.   Autocratic
    C.   Operating   D.   Staff

22. Performance evaluations that are conducted more often than quarterly will probably be   22.____
    most useful to organizations that

    A.   are in relatively unstable environments
    B.   are focused on long-term growth
    C.   tend to have older employees
    D.   rely heavily on sales personnel

23. In formulating a pay structure, the most crucial factor is the   23.____

    A.   number of different jobs
    B.   numerical ratio between management and labor positions
    C.   size of differentials among jobs
    D.   pay level of competitors

24. Among the following, the type of performance evaluation most rarely used involves   24.____
    assessment by

    A.   peers   B.   superiors only
    C.   subordinates   D.   self-evaluation

25. When a new employee is required to be a union member when hired, a(n) _____ situa-   25.____
    tion exists.

    A. agency shop   B. closed shop
    C. certified   D. union shop

———————

KEY (CORRECT ANSWERS)

1.	C	11.	D
2.	D	12.	C
3.	B	13.	B
4.	A	14.	A
5.	B	15.	B
6.	C	16.	D
7.	B	17.	C
8.	D	18.	C
9.	D	19.	A
10.	C	20.	B

21.	D
22.	A
23.	C
24.	A
25.	B

———————

TEST 2

DIRECTIONS: Each question or incomplete statement is followed by several suggested answers or completions. Select the one that BEST answers the question or completes the statement. *PRINT THE LETTER OF THE CORRECT ANSWER IN THE SPACE AT THE RIGHT.*

1. The main difference between replacement planning and succession planning is that   1.____

    A. replacement planning does not take an employee's age into account
    B. succession planning is more broadly applied and integrated
    C. replacement planning is used primarily with nontechnical labor positions
    D. succession planning merely specifies individual replacements for specific jobs

2. Under the provisions of the Americans with Disabilities Act, each of the following practices is prohibited EXCEPT   2.____

    A. participating in contractual arrangements that discriminate against the disabled
    B. limiting the advancement opportunities of disabled employees
    C. firing an employee whose disability diminishes or limits performance of a particular job
    D. using tests or job requirements that tend to screen out the disabled

3. In the overall union structure, the roles of a national union typically include each of the following EXCEPT   3.____

    A. establishing the rules and policies under which local unions may be chartered
    B. exercising a degree of control over the collection of dues and the admission of members
    C. providing the local unions with support for organizing campaigns and administering contracts
    D. providing office space and other facilities for local unions

4. Which of the following is TRUE of multi-skilled pay structures?   4.____

    A. They typically involve clerical employees.
    B. When used, they typically involve about 80% of a company's workforce.
    C. They are most common among large facilities (over 500 employees).
    D. Managerial or supervisory employees are almost never included.

5. Which of the following states has in effect *right-to-work* laws that ban any form of compulsory union membership?   5.____

    A. Ohio   B. California
    C. Texas   D. New York

6. The Employment Retirement Income Security Act (ERISA) does NOT   6.____

    A. cover multi-employer benefit plans
    B. establish minimum eligibility requirements for existing private pension plans
    C. require an employer to establish a private pension plan
    D. require an employer to disclose to employees the details of a private pension plan

7. In supervising employees, a manager usually keeps a written record of unusual incidents   7.____
that show both positive and negative actions by an employee. What is the term for such a
record?

    A. Critical-incident appraisal
    B. Exception record
    C. Forced-choice rating
    D. Deviation journal

8. Which of the following methods for forecasting an organization's demand for employees   8.____
is usually the LEAST mathematically sophisticated?

    A. Unit demand forecasting   B. Modeling
    C. Expert estimate   D. Trend projection

9. Which of the following federal laws established the National Labor Relations Board   9.____
(NLRB)?

    A. Norris-LaGuardia Act   B. Wagner Act
    C. Taft-Hartley Act   D. Landrum-Griffin Act

10. Which of the following is a legal way for an organization's management to prevent a   10.____
union from organizing?

    A. Providing wages and fringe benefits that make union membership unattractive
    B. Dismissing employees who want to unionize
    C. Promising rewards if a union is voted down
    D. None of the above

11. The main advantage associated with flextime scheduling methods is that the need for   11.____
_____ is minimized.

    A. maternity leave   B. personal time off
    C. sick days   D. family leave

12. Which of the following types of labor strikes is considered illegal because it constitutes   12.____
an invasion of private property?

    A. Wildcat   B. Sitdown
    C. Jurisdictional   D. Economic

13. If the primary purpose of a performance evaluation method is development, and costs   13.____
are to be a consideration, which of the following methods is most appropriate?

    A. Essay evaluation
    B. Management by objectives (MBO)
    C. Behavioral observation scales (BOS)
    D. Paired comparison

14. Currently, the erosion of union power in the U.S. labor market rests on each of the follow-　14.____
ing factors EXCEPT

    A.　a decrease in demand by nonunionized employees for union representation
    B.　a shift in the workforce from blue-collar manufacturing workers to better-paid ser-
vice and knowledge workers
    C.　the increasing protections already afforded U.S. laborers by federal labor legisla-
tion
    D.　increased product market competitiveness in a global market

15. Of all the different kinds of benefits and services that can be offered to employees, the　15.____
least preferred seem to be

    A.　child care
    B.　life insurance
    C.　social and recreational programs
    D.　educational programs

16. When labor and management are in conflict on a common problem, and when the out-　16.____
come is a win/win situation, _____ bargaining is said to be occurring.

    A.　distributive   B.　differential
    C.　integrative   D.　collective

17. According to the provisions of the Civil Rights Act of 1991, a plaintiff who sues an organi-　17.____
zation for intentional hiring or workplace discrimination is limited to a damages cap of
_____ if the organization employs between 100 and 200 people.

    A.　$50,000   B.　$100,000   C.　$200,000   D.　$300,000

18. Which of the following is generally TRUE of an autocratic leader and the group in his or　18.____
her charge?

    A.　Production is usually low in the leader's absence.
    B.　The leader does not set goals for the group.
    C.　A feeling of responsibility is developed within the group.
    D.　Quality of work is generally high.

19. Which of the following is NOT a typical feature of a programmed instruction training pro-　19.____
gram?

    A.　The learner receives immediate feedback on her progress.
    B.　Instruction is provided under the supervision of a human instructor.
    C.　Behaviorist learning principles are followed closely.
    D.　The learner learns at her own rate.

20. Which of the following groups of employees is most at risk for alcoholism?   20._____

    A. Those aged 20-30 who do not have families
    B. Those aged 25-40 who have made many lateral moves within a single organization
    C. Those aged 35-55 who have been employed at the same enterprise for 14-20 years
    D. Older employees (55-65) nearing retirement who have worked with a company for most of their lives

21. Which of the following performance evaluation methods is most useful for the purpose of counseling and development of employees?   21._____

    A. Paired comparison
    B. Ranking
    C. Graphic rating scale
    D. Management by objectives (MBO)

22. In human resources management, *routing* refers to   22._____

    A. the assignment of tasks to newly hired employees
    B. an employee's promotion through the company hierarchy
    C. determining the best sequence of operations
    D. the elimination of unnecessary or unproductive employees

23. Which of the following needs assessment techniques, conducted prior to implementation of a training program, is the most time-consuming?   23._____

    A. Advisory committees   B. Group discussion
    C. Assessment centers   D. Skills testing

24. At a certain school district, a bachelor's degree in education places a teacher at *step one* on the salary scale. An additional nine semester hours of college coursework earns an increase of $400. This is an example of a   24._____

    A. skill-based pay structure
    B. knowledge-based pay structure
    C. pay level determined by internal competitiveness
    D. pay level determined by external competitiveness

25. Which of the following is considered a health hazard rather than a safety hazard?   25._____

    A. Exposure to hazardous chemicals
    B. Unsafe machinery
    C. Biological hazards
    D. Poorly maintained equipment

KEY (CORRECT ANSWERS)

1.	B	11.	B
2.	C	12.	B
3.	D	13.	A
4.	D	14.	C
5.	C	15.	C
6.	C	16.	C
7.	A	17.	B
8.	C	18.	A
9.	B	19.	B
10.	A	20.	C

21.	D
22.	C
23.	D
24.	B
25.	C

———

EXAMINATION SECTION
TEST 1

DIRECTIONS: Each question or incomplete statement is followed by several suggested answers or completions. Select the one that BEST answers the question or completes the statement. *PRINT THE LETTER OF THE CORRECT ANSWER IN THE SPACE AT THE RIGHT.*

1. Willful violations of OSHA provisions by a corporate employer are punishable by maximum fines of up to_____ upon criminal conviction.   1._____

    A. $5,000   B. $50,000   C. $250,000   D. $500,000

2. Which of the following occurs when employees perceive too narrow a difference between their own pay and that of other colleagues?   2._____

    A. Pay compression   B. Wage inflation
    C. Pay survey   D. Skills gap

3. A local union typically engages in each of the following activities EXCEPT   3._____

    A. administering contracts   B. training union leaders
    C. organizing campaigns   D. collecting dues

4. Under existing laws or mandates, affirmative action programs are mandated for the hiring practices of   4._____

    A. public educational institutions
    B. government contractors
    C. federal agencies
    D. all of the above

5. In evaluating a training program, a human resources professional wants specifically to learn whether the knowledge, skills, or abilities learned in training led to an employee's improved performance on the job. Her evaluation of the program would test for _____ validity.   5._____

    A. training   B. transfer
    C. intraorganizational   D. interorganizational

6. In human resources, *methods study* is concerned with   6._____

    A. the way in which work is distributed among personnel
    B. determining the most efficient way of doing a task or job
    C. determining the minimum number of employees needed to complete a task or job
    D. the criteria used to hire employees

7. Which of the following is/are advantages associated with internal recruiting?   7._____
    I.   It offers loyal employees a fair chance at promotion.
    II. It helps protect trade secrets.
    III. It encourages new ideas and competition.
    The CORRECT answer is:

    A. I *only*   B. III *only*   C. I, II   D. II, III

8. In the vocabulary of job analysis, coordinated and aggregated series of work elements   8._____
that are used to produce a specific output are referred to as

    A. positions   B. jobs   C. chores   D. tasks

9. During the personnel selection process, human resource professionals sometimes use   9._____
selection tests that are designed to have what is called *predictive validity.* The primary
drawback to using this type of assessment is that

    A. employees are often unwilling to take extensive test batteries
    B. an employer must wait until a large enough *predictive* group has been hired to
        norm the measurement
    C. *self-selection* bias can restrict the range of test scores
    D. results are often skewed toward applicants with previous experience

10. Jobs whose salaries are below the minimum of the salary range for the job are described   10._____
as _____ jobs.

    A. broadband   B. red circle
    C. green circle   D. exempt

11. In an organization with a human resources department, which of the following informa-   11._____
tion is most likely to be covered by the operating supervisor in orienting a new employee?

    A. A brief history of the organization
    B. Rules, regulations, policies, and procedures
    C. Personnel policies
    D. Reviewing performance criteria

12. In human resources management, *pay structure* refers to   12._____

    A. pay set relative to employees working on different jobs within the organization
    B. a grouping of a variety of work jobs that are similar in their difficulty and responsi-
        bility requirements
    C. pay set relative to employees working on similar jobs in other organizations
    D. a survey of the compensation of all employees by all employers in a geographic
        area, an industry, or an occupational group

13. Which of the following is a provision of the Rehabilitation Act, as amended?   13._____

    A. Employers may not cite the potential legal liability for drug-related injuries or acci-
        dents as a reason for firing an employee.
    B. Employers of 100 or more must establish employee assistance programs (EAPs)
        for helping drug addicts or alcoholics to recover.
    C. Employers of any size may not fire, or refuse to hire, an employee or candidate
        solely because of alcohol or drug addiction.
    D. Drug addiction and alcoholism are not be be considered *disabilities* in the same
        category as other employee handicaps.

14. A disadvantage of using ranking as a job evaluation method is that   14._____

    A. it is the slowest of all job evaluation methods
    B. it requires cumbersome descriptions of each job class
    C. it is one of the more expensive methods
    D. its results are nearly always more subjective than with other methods

15. In an organization that employs at least some union members, union members are sometimes given preferences over nonunion members in areas such as hiring, promotion, and layoff. Preferences given in this situation are often likely to violate the provisions of the _____ Act.

    A. Taft-Hartley   B. Wagner
    C. Landrum-Griffin   D. Fair Labor Standards

15._____

16. In human resources management, the _____ principle states that authority flows one link at a time, from the top of the organization to the bottom.

    A. parity   B. scalar   C. quality   D. graduation

16._____

17. When an employee training program fails, the most common reason is that

    A. training needs changed after the program had been implemented
    B. employees were not motivated
    C. there were no on-the-job rewards for behaviors and skills learned in training
    D. there were inaccurate training needs analyses

17._____

18. In implementing a progressive discipline pattern with a difficult employee, the first step is typically to

    A. issue a written warning to the employee
    B. impose a period of *decision leave* for the employee to consider his or her actions
    C. enroll the employee in additional training
    D. counsel or discuss the problem with the employee

18._____

19. The most widely used method of career planning that occurs in organizations is

    A. the planning workshop
    B. the extended seminar
    C. the self-assessment center
    D. counseling by supervisors and human resources staff

19._____

20. Under the provisions of the Equal Pay Act, differences in _____ is NOT a justification for paying a man more than a woman for the same job.

    A. performance   B. skill
    C. family situations   D. seniority

20._____

21. Compensation plans that protect the wages of workers hired before a certain date but start new workers at a lower pay rate are described as

    A. straight piecework   B. weighted
    C. two-tiered   D. differential piece rate

21._____

22. To prevent bias and legal complications, performance evaluations should steer clear of each of the following traits EXCEPT

    A. dependability   B. knowledge
    C. attitude   D. drive

22._____

23. The type of benefits most valued by employees are typically

    A. paid vacation and holidays
    B. medical
    C. long–term disability
    D. dental

23.____

24. Which of the following is the most common reason for employees to be opposed to the process of performance evaluation?

    A. Interference with normal work patterns
    B. Operating problems
    C. Bad system design
    D. Rater subjectivity

24.____

25. _____ training is most commonly used in the workplace.

    A. Apprenticeship   B. Vestibule
    C. Cross-   D. Classroom

25.____

KEY (CORRECT ANSWERS)

1.	D		11.	D
2.	A		12.	A
3.	B		13.	B
4.	B		14.	D
5.	B		15.	A
6.	B		16.	B
7.	C		17.	C
8.	D		18.	D
9.	B		19.	D
10.	C		20.	C

21.	C
22.	B
23.	B
24.	D
25.	D

TEST 2

DIRECTIONS: Each question or incomplete statement is followed by several suggested answers or completions. Select the one that BEST answers the question or completes the statement. *PRINT THE LETTER OF THE CORRECT ANSWER IN THE SPACE AT THE RIGHT.*

1. In today's personnel market, the most critical factor used by recruiters to evaluate pro-   1.____
   spective job candidates who hold an MBA is usually the

   A. institution from which the degree was earned
   B. applicant's interpersonal style
   C. applicant's demonstrated skill level
   D. applicant's previous work experience

2. If a human resources manager decides to implement a preventive health care program in   2.____
   the workplace, he or she should be careful to guard against

   A. an increase in the number of medical claims made by employees
   B. a lack of quantifiable proof that the program is saving money or increasing produc-
      tivity
   C. the splintering of the wellness program into its own budgetary status
   D. the abuse of available resources by employees

3. Competition is most likely to be a problem in performance evaluations that involve rating   3.____
   by

   A. the employee's subordinates
   B. the employee's peers
   C. self-evaluation
   D. a committee of several supervisors

4. Which of the following is not a problem commonly associated with merit pay systems?   4.____

   A. Employees often fail to make the connection between pay and performance.
   B. The size of merit awards has little effect on performance.
   C. Costs are usually higher than in individual incentive plans.
   D. The secrecy of rewards is seen as inequity by employees.

5. Which of the following step in the job analysis process is typically performed FIRST?   5.____

   A. Collecting data
   B. Selecting the jobs to be analyzed
   C. Determining how job analysis information will be used
   D. Preparing job descriptions

6. In which of the following sectors are employees typically most expensive to train?   6.____

   A. Consumer products
   B. Agriculture/forestry/fishing
   C. Services
   D. Industrial products

7. A commonly encountered disadvantage of using Bureau of Labor Statistics (BLS) data in pay surveys is that they

    A. tend to skew data in a way that favors labor over management
    B. are too generalized to be useful
    C. only list maximum and minimum pay rates, not medians and averages
    D. are not widely available to the public

7.____

8. Other than the salaries of training staff and trainees, which of the following is typically the largest expense involved in conducting an employee training program?

    A. Seminars and conferences
    B. Outside services
    C. Facilities and overhead
    D. Hardware

8.____

9. Under the provisions of the Equal Pay Act, differences in pay for equal work are permitted if they result from any of the following EXCEPT differences in

    A. seniority
    B. quality of performance
    C. age
    D. quantity or quality of production

9.____

10. Which of the following personnel selection procedures is typically LEAST costly?

    A. Background and reference checks
    B. Employment interview
    C. Preliminary screening
    D. Employment tests

10.____

11. Which of the following is a strictly internal method of personnel recruitment?

    A. Employment agencies
    B. Recruitment advertising
    C. Special-events recruiting
    D. Job posting

11.____

12. Of the following individual performance evaluation techniques, which has the advantage of offering the flexibility to discuss what the organization is attempting to accomplish?

    A. Graphic rating scale
    B. Behaviorally anchored rating scale (BARS)
    C. Essay evaluation
    D. Behavioral observation scale (BOS)

12.____

13. In human resources management, the *Pygmalion effect* refers to the tendency of an employee to

    A. live up to a manager's expectations
    B. identify with a working group
    C. sacrifice his or her personal life for improved work performance
    D. avoid work if at all possible

13.____

14. In medium-sized and larger organizations, the role of a human resources manager in the   14._____
selection process is most often characterized by

    A. conducting the selection interview
    B. narrowing a field of applicants to a smaller, more manageable number
    C. designing the process by which candidates will be selected
    D. exercising final authority for hiring decisions

15. Employees who believe they have been discriminated against under the *whistleblowing*   15._____
provisions of the Occupational Safety and Health Act may file a complaint at the nearest
OSHA office within _____ of the alleged discriminatory action.

    A. 10 days   B. 30 days   C. 90 days   D. 6 months

16. Of the many applications possible with computerized human resource information sys-   16._____
tems, which of the following is most commonly used?

    A. Equal employment opportunity records
    B. Job analysis
    C. Performance appraisals
    D. Career pathing

17. _____ cost(s) is the term for expenditures for necessary items that do not become a part   17._____
of a product or service.

    A. Operating supplies   B. Overhead
    C. Maintenance   D. Material

18. The union official who is responsible for representing the interests of local members in   18._____
their relations with managers on the job is the

    A. president   B. business representative
    C. committee person   D. vice president

19. Of the many types of employment tests used in personnel selection, _____ tests tend to   19._____
have the highest validities and reliabilities.

    A. performance simulation
    B. paper-and-pencil
    C. job sample performance
    D. personality and temperament

20. If an employee exhibits a *behavior discrepancy*—if his or her performance varies from   20._____
what is expected on the job—a human resources manager might conduct a performance
analysis. Most of these analyses begin with the process of

    A. motivating the employee to do better
    B. setting clear standards for performance on the job
    C. training the employee
    D. conducting a cost/value analysis of correcting the identified behavior

21. It is NOT a common goal of the orientation process to

    A. reduce personnel turnover   B. reduce anxiety
    C. develop realistic expectations   D. teach an employee specific job skills

21._____

22. In order for a situation to be accurately described as a job *layoff*, each of the following conditions must occur EXCEPT

    A. there is no work available
    B. the work shortage is sudden and surprising
    C. management expects the no-work situation to be temporary
    D. management intends to recall the employee

22._____

23. In a(n) _____ payroll plan, pay is based on two separate piecework rates: one for those who produce below or up to standard, and another for those who produce up to standard.

    A. equity   B. Taylor
    C. functional   D. distributive

23._____

24. Approximately what percentage of the U.S. labor force is currently unionized?

    A. 5   B. 15   C. 45   D. 70

24._____

25. The _____ principle states that managers should concentrate their efforts on matters that deviate from the normal and let their employees handle routine matters.

    A. critical-incident   B. flow-process   C. exception   D. democratic

25._____

KEY (CORRECT ANSWERS)

1. B		11. D	
2. B		12. C	
3. B		13. A	
4. C		14. B	
5. C		15. B	
6. D		16. A	
7. B		17. A	
8. C		18. C	
9. C		19. C	
10. C		20. D	

21.	D
22.	B
23.	B
24.	B
25.	C

EXAMINATION SECTION
TEST 1

DIRECTIONS: Each question or incomplete statement is followed by several suggested answers or completions. Select the one that BEST answers the question or completes the statement. *PRINT THE LETTER OF THE CORRECT ANSWER IN THE SPACE AT THE RIGHT.*

1. Which of the following items of federal legislation was designed to encourage the growth of labor unions and restrain management from interfering with that growth?

    A. Wagner Act
    B. Taft–Hartley Act
    C. Fair Labor Standards Act
    D. Sherman Antitrust Act

1.____

2. The _____ training approach to employee training involves a simulation of the real working environment.

    A. apprenticeship   B. classroom
    C. vestibule   D. step

2.____

3. Company A is conducting a wage survey in order to determine its external competitiveness. In order to be useful and informative, the survey results must include each of the following EXCEPT

    A. the names and sizes of the companies surveyed
    B. a brief description of job duties
    C. data from companies that are in the same geographic location
    D. the dates on which listed wages and salaries were in effect

3.____

4. In forecasting an organization's demand for employees, which of the following is a *bottom–up* technique?

    A. Trend projection   B. Unit demand forecasting
    C. Modeling   D. Expert estimate

4.____

5. What is the term for the method in which a manager continually ranks his or her employees from most valuable to least valuable?

    A. Object classification   B. Alteration ranking
    C. Subject categorization   D. Forced–choice rating

5.____

6. In order to be effective, the criteria on which performance evaluations are based should be designed with each of the following in mind EXCEPT

    A. relevance   B. practicality
    C. comprehensiveness   D. sensitivity

6.____

7. Historically, the personnel function was considered to be concerned almost exclusively with blue–collar or operating employees, until about the

    A. 1890s   B. 1920s   C. 1960s   D. 1990s

7.____

8. During an employment interview, the solicitation of information about _____, in ANY situation, no matter what the perceived relationship to the job, is unlawful.   8._____

    A. religion
    C. race or color
    B. handicaps
    D. national origin

9. What is the term for the process of unionized employees voting to drop the union?   9._____

    A. Decertification
    C. Exposure
    B. Opening shop
    D. Closing shop

10. All written sexual harassment policies presented by an employer need to contain the following EXCEPT a(n)   10._____

    A. statement encouraging people to come forward with complaints
    B. definition of sexual harassment
    C. alternative channel for filing complaints
    D. promise to make a case public once it has been confirmed and resolved

11. To human resource professionals, the primary advantage associated with computer–aided job evaluations is that they   11._____

    A. decrease the bureaucratic burdens associated with the process
    B. produce results that are more widely accepted
    C. are much more efficient than other kinds of processes
    D. are nearly always less expensive than other methods

12. In order for the National Labor Relations Board to be appropriately petitioned to hold a representation election to determine whether employees in a bargaining unit can be represented by a union, at least _____% of the bargaining unit's employees must sign an authorization card.   12._____

    A. 10   B. 30   C. 50   D. 75

13. Which of the following items of federal legislation was designed to audit and regulate the internal affairs of unions?   13._____

    A. Civil Rights Act of 1964
    B. Landrum–Griffin Act
    C. Fair Labor Standards Act
    D. Robinson–Patman Act

14. Which of the following unions is currently experiencing the most rapid growth rate?   14._____

    A. Service Employees International Union
    B. United Steel Workers
    C. American Federation of Government Employees
    D. United Auto Workers

15. Which of the following is NOT a potential disadvantage associated with a flexible–bene-   15._____
fits plan?

    A. It requires intensive administrative effort.
    B. It often results in erratic cost patterns for the organization.
    C. For employees, contributions and deductibles are often increased.
    D. It tends to raise the costs of introducing new forms of benefits.

16. Under the Hazard Communications Standard of the Occupational Safety and Health Act,   16._____
either of the following may complete Material Safety Data Sheets on chemicals imported
into, produced, or used in the workplace EXCEPT

    A. employees   B. manufacturers
    C. employers   D. importers

17. The term *halo effect* is most often used to refer to cases when a human resources man-   17._____
ager

    A. allows a single prominent characteristic of an interviewee to dominate judgment of
all other characteristics
    B. projects the behaviors and attitudes of one prominent employee onto other
employees
    C. typifies an employee's work habits by one exceptional example, good or bad
    D. considers all of the employees in his or her charge together as one unit, rather than
as individuals

18. Approximately how much time should be scheduled by a human resources department   18._____
to develop a behaviorally anchored rating scale (BARS) for performance evaluation?

    A. 1 working day   B. 2–4 days
    C. 2 weeks   D. 6 weeks

19. Each of the following actions, if taken by a human resources manager, is likely to have a   19._____
positive effect on employee motivation EXCEPT

    A. treating employees as members of a group
    B. encouraging participation
    C. relating rewards to performance
    D. making work interesting

20. Which of the following federal laws prohibited a union to require that a person be a mem-   20._____
ber of a union before he or she is hired?

    A. Sherman Antitrust Act   B. Clayton Act
    C. Taft–Hartley Act   D. Landrum–Griffin Act

21. Among the different types of retirement plans, 401(k) plans are classified as   21._____

    A. employee stock ownership plans (ESOPs)
    B. private pensions
    C. tax reduction stock ownership plans (TRASOPs)
    D. asset income

22. The strictness of a company's employee discipline policy depends most on 22.____

    A. the supportiveness of the work group
    B. the nature of the supervisor
    C. the nature of the prevailing labor markets
    D. existing legal statutes

23. The first union in the United States to achieve significant size and influence was the 23.____

    A. United Garment Workers
    B. American Federation of Labor
    C. Knights of Labor
    D. Congress of Industrial Organizations

24. What is the term for a diagram which vertically represents the activities to be performed, 24.____
and horizontally represents the time required to perform them?

    A. Nomograph   B. Gantt chart
    C. Layout chart   D. Flow–process chart

25. The age discrimination provisions of the Age Discrimination in Employment Act apply to 25.____
all employers of _____ or more people.

    A. 5   B. 15   C. 20   D. 100

KEY (CORRECT ANSWERS)

1.	A		11.	A
2.	C		12.	B
3.	A		13.	B
4.	B		14.	A
5.	B		15.	D
6.	C		16.	A
7.	C		17.	A
8.	C		18.	B
9.	A		19.	A
10.	A		20.	C

21.	D
22.	C
23.	C
24.	B
25.	C

TEST 2

DIRECTIONS: Each question or incomplete statement is followed by several suggested answers or completions. Select the one that BEST answers the question or completes the statement. *PRINT THE LETTER OF THE CORRECT ANSWER IN THE SPACE AT THE RIGHT.*

1. Which of the following is NOT a disadvantage commonly associated with skill–based pay structures?

   A. They often result in bloated staffing.
   B. Their compliance with the Equal Pay Act is still undecided on many points.
   C. They are based mostly on job content.
   D. They often become expensive if not properly managed.

   1.____

2. The number of applicants hired at an organization, divided by the total number of applicants, yields a statistic known as a _____ ratio.

   A. turnover   B. market pay
   C. selection   D. recruitment success

   2.____

3. Job _____ is the term for the formal process by which the relative worth of various jobs in the organization is determined for pay purposes.

   A. analysis   B. specification
   C. evaluation   D. enlargement

   3.____

4. Which of the following is NOT an effective means of counteracting commonly–occurring career problems in a new employee?

   A. Give the employee a challenging initial assignment
   B. De–emphasize a job's negative aspects
   C. Give the employee as much authority as possible
   D. Assign new employees initially to demanding supervisors

   4.____

5. In the factor comparison method of job evaluation, which of the following is typically performed LAST?

   A. Benchmark or key jobs are evaluated according to compensable factors.
   B. Key jobs are displayed in a job comparison chart.
   C. Comparison factors are selected and defined.
   D. Evaluators allocate a part of each key job's wage to each job factor.

   5.____

6. Concerning discipline, employees _____ are usually the easiest to work with and adjust.

   A. with alcohol–or drug–related problems
   B. whose performance are due to factors directly related to work
   C. whose performance are due to problems caused by the work group
   D. with family problems

   6.____

7. Among individual performance assessment techniques, the oldest and most commonly used is the

   A. critical incident technique
   B. forced–choice evaluation
   C. weighted checklist
   D. graphic rating scale

   7.____

8. The *traditional* theory of human resources management holds that _____ is the primary   8._____
    motivator of people.

    A. money   B. approval
    C. achievement   D. safety

9. Generally, under the child labor provisions of the Fair Labor Standards Act, children must   9._____
    be at LEAST _____ years old to be employed in interstate commerce of any kind.

    A. 12   B. 14   C. 16   D. 18

10. Benefits are typically evaluated by human resource professionals in terms of their objec-   10._____
    tives. Which of the following objectives tends to be LEAST important in these evalua-
    tions?

    A. Impact on employee families
    B. Fairness or equity with which they are viewed by employees
    C. Cost effectiveness of benefit decisions
    D. Impact on employee work behaviors

11. Which of the following performance assessment techniques tends to involve the highest   11._____
    developmental costs?

    A. Graphic rating scale
    B. Performance testing
    C. Field review
    D. Management by objectives (MBO)

12. Which of the following types of employees is NOT typically classified as *exempt* under   12._____
    the Fair Labor Standards Act?

    A. Line workers   B. Administrators
    C. Outside sales personnel   D. Executives

13. Which of the following is a typical guideline to be followed in the process of orienting a   13._____
    new employee to the workplace?

    A. The most significant part of orientation deals with necessary job skills and work
        habits, rather than the nature of the relationship between the new employee and
        supervisors and/or co–workers.
    B. New employees should be allowed a generous amount of time to adjust to the new
        workplace before their responsibilities are increased.
    C. New employees should be *sponsored* or directed in the immediate environment by
        a group of experienced workers.
    D. Orientation should begin with the more general policies of the organization.

14. The _____ theory of employee motivation is based on the assumption that employees   14._____
    are motivated to satisfy a number of needs and that money can satisfy, directly or indi-
    rectly, only some of these needs.

    A. traditional
    B. behavioral/reinforcement
    C. need hierarchy
    D. achievement–power–affiliation

15. Which of the following is a grouping of a variety of jobs that are similar in terms of work difficulty and responsibility?   15._____

    A. Pay class   B. Job classification
    C. Broadband   D. Rate change

16. Which of the following statements is TRUE of recruitment that is performed using realistic job previews (RJPs)?   16._____

    A. RJPs tend to reduce the flow of highly capable applicants into the organization.
    B. RJPs tend to generate an extremely high rate of job offer acceptance.
    C. RJPs make a job look unattractive to some or many applicants.
    D. Employees hired after receiving RJPs tend to have a lower rate of job survival than those using traditional previews.

17. The theory of human behavior based on the belief that people attempt to increase pleasure and decrease displeasure is the _____ theory.   17._____

    A. input–output
    B. achievement–power–affiliation
    C. preference–expectancy
    D. behavioral

18. The agencies most responsible for enforcing equal employment opportunity regulations include each of the following EXCEPT the   18._____

    A. Occupational Health and Safety Administration (OSHA)
    B. Equal Employment Opportunity Commission (EEOC)
    C. federal courts
    D. Office of Federal Contract Compliance Programs (OFCCP)

19. The majority of top–level managers consider _____ as the most important workplace activity for dealing with employee substance abuse.   19._____

    A. employee assistance programs
    B. drug testing
    C. supervisory training programs
    D. drug education programs

20. In the performance evaluation process, which of the following functions is typically undertaken exclusively by the human resource manager, rather than the operating manager?   20._____

    A. Training the raters
    B. Setting the policy on evaluation criteria
    C. Discussing the evaluation with the employee
    D. Choosing the evaluation system

21. Which of the following characteristics is LEAST likely to influence the acceptance of vari-   21.____
able pay plans by employees of an organization?

    A. Ratio of variable pay to base pay (leverage)
    B. Amount of base pay
    C. Risk
    D. Procedural justice

22. Which of the following is a performance simulation test used in the personnel selection   22.____
process?

    A. Wonderlic Personnel Test
    B. Wechsler Adult Intelligence Scale
    C. California Test of Mental Maturity
    D. Revised Minnesota Paper Form Board Test

23. The extent to which a technique for selecting employees is successful in predicting   23.____
important elements of job behavior is known as

    A. construct validity   B. job correlation
    C. normative probability   D. criterion–related validity

24. Critics of the *rotation and transfer* method of on–the–job training for managers argue that   24.____
this method

    A. creates generalists who may not be able to manage in many specialized situations
    B. discourages new ideas in the work environment
    C. does not provide authentic work experiences
    D. slows the promotion of highly competent individuals

25. According to the Theory X/Theory Y concept of leadership attitudes, which of the follow-   25.____
ing is a Theory X assumption?

    A. Commitment to objectives is a function of the rewards associated with their
        achievement.
    B. The average person learns, under proper conditions, not only to accept but to seek
        responsibility.
    C. Under the conditions of modern industrial life, the intellectual potentials of the aver-
        age person are only partially utilized.
    D. The average person prefers to be directed.

KEY (CORRECT ANSWERS)

1.	A		11.	B
2.	C		12.	A
3.	C		13.	B
4.	B		14.	C
5.	B		15.	A
6.	B		16.	C
7.	D		17.	C
8.	A		18.	A
9.	C		19.	A
10.	A		20.	A

21.	B
22.	D
23.	D
24.	A
25.	D

———

EXAMINATION SECTION
TEST 1

DIRECTIONS: Each question or incomplete statement is followed by several suggested answers or completions. Select the one that BEST answers the question or completes the statement. *PRINT THE LETTER OF THE CORRECT ANSWER IN THE SPACE AT THE RIGHT.*

1. Deviant behavior is a sociological term used to describe behavior which is not in accord with generally accepted standards. This may include juvenile delinquency, adult criminality, mental or physical illness.
   Comparison of normal with deviant behavior is useful to social workers because it

   A. makes it possible to establish watertight behavioral descriptions
   B. provides evidence of differential social behavior which distinguishes deviant from normal behavior
   C. indicates that deviant behavior is of no concern to social workers
   D. provides no evidence that social role is a determinant of behavior

   1._____

2. Alcoholism may affect an individual client's ability to function as a spouse, parent, worker, and citizen.
   A social worker's MAIN responsibility to a client with a history of alcoholism is to

   A. interpret to the client the causes of alcoholism as a disease syndrome
   B. work with the alcoholic's family to accept him as he is and stop trying to reform him
   C. encourage the family of the alcoholic to accept casework treatment
   D. determine the origins of his particular drinking problem, establish a diagnosis, and work out a treatment plan for him

   2._____

3. There is a trend to regard narcotic addiction as a form of illness for which the current methods of intervention have not been effective.
   Research on the combination of social, psychological, and physical causes of addiction would indicate that social workers should

   A. oppose hospitalization of addicts in institutions
   B. encourage the addict to live normally at home
   C. recognize that there is no successful treatment for addiction and act accordingly
   D. use the existing community facilities differentially for each addict

   3._____

4. A study of social relationships among delinquent and non-delinquent youth has shown that

   A. delinquent youth generally conceal their true feelings and maintain furtive social contacts
   B. delinquents are more impulsive and vivacious than law-abiding boys
   C. non-delinquent youths diminish their active social relationships in order to sublimate any anti-social impulses
   D. delinquent and non-delinquent youths exhibit similar characteristics of impulsiveness and vivaciousness

   4._____

5. The one of the following which is the CHIEF danger of interpreting the delinquent behav-   5.____
   ior of a child in terms of morality *alone* when attempting to get at its causes is that

   A. this tends to overlook the likelihood that the causes of the child's actions are more
      than a negation of morality and involve varied symptoms of disturbance
   B. a child's moral outlook toward life and society is largely colored by that of his par-
      ents, thus encouraging parent-child conflict
   C. too careful a consideration of the moral aspects of the offense and of the child's
      needs may often negate the demands of justice in a case
   D. standards of morality may be of no concern to the delinquent and he may not real-
      ize the seriousness of his offenses

6. Experts in the field of personnel administration are generally agreed that an employee   6.____
   should not be under the immediate supervision of more than one supervisor. A certain
   worker, because of an emergency situation, divides his time equally between two limited
   caseloads on a prearranged time schedule. Each unit has a different supervisor, and the
   worker performs substantially the same duties in each caseload.
   The above statement is pertinent in this situation CHIEFLY because

   A. each supervisor, feeling that the cases in her unit should have priority, may
      demand too much of the worker's time
   B. the two supervisors may have different standards of work performance and may
      prefer different methods of doing the work
   C. the worker works part-time on each caseload and may not have full knowledge or
      control of the situation in either caseload
   D. the task of evaluating the worker's services will be doubled, with two supervisors
      instead of one having to rate his work

7. Experts in modern personnel management generally agree that employees on all job lev-   7.____
   els should be permitted to offer suggestions for improving work methods.
   Of the following, the CHIEF limitation of such suggestions is that they may, at times,

   A. be offered primarily for financial reward and not show genuine interest in improve-
      ment of work methods
   B. be directed towards making individual jobs easier
   C. be restricted by the employees' fear of radically changing the work methods
      favored by their supervisors
   D. show little awareness of the effects on the overall objectives and functions of the
      entire agency

8. Through the supervisory process and relationship, the supervisor is trying to help work-   8.____
   ers gain increased self-awareness.
   Of the following statements concerning this process, the one which is MOST accurate
   is:

   A. Self-awareness is developed gradually so that worker can learn to control his own
      reactions.
   B. Worker is expected to be introspective primarily for his own enlightenment.
   C. Supervisor is trying to help worker handle any emotional difficulties he may reveal.
   D. Worker is expected at the onset to share and determine with the supervisor what in
      his previous background makes it difficult for him to use certain ideas.

9. The one of the following statements concerning principles in the learning process which is LEAST accurate is: 9.____

   A. Some degree of regression on the part of the worker is usually natural in the process of development and this should be accepted by the supervisor.
   B. When a beginning worker shows problems, the supervisor should first handle this behavior as a personality difficulty.
   C. It has been found in the work training process that some degree of resistance is usually inevitable.
   D. The emotional content of work practice may tend to set up *blind spots* in workers.

10. Of the following, the one that represents the BEST basis for planning the content of a successful staff development program is the 10.____

   A. time available for meetings
   B. chief social problems of the community
   C. common needs of the staff workers as related to the situations with which they are dealing
   D. experimental programs conducted by other agencies

11. In planning staff development seminars, the MOST valuable topics for discussion are likely to be those selected from 11.____

   A. staff suggestions based on the staff's interest and needs
   B. topics recommended for consideration by professional organizations
   C. topics selected by the administration based on demonstrated limitations of staff skill and knowledge
   D. topics selected by the administration based on a combination of staff interest and objectivity evaluated staff needs

12. Staff meetings designed to promote professional staff development are MOST likely to achieve this goal when 12.____

   A. there is the widest participation among all staff members who attend the meetings
   B. participation by the most skilled and experienced staff members is predominant
   C. participation by selected staff members is planned before the meeting sessions
   D. supervisory personnel take major responsibility for participation

13. Assume that you are the leader of a conference attended by representatives of various city and private agencies. After the conference has been underway for a considerable time, you realize that the representative of one of these agencies has said nothing. It would generally be BEST for you to 13.____

   A. ask him if he would like to say anything
   B. ask the group a pertinent question that he would probably be best able to answer
   C. make no special effort to include him in the conversation
   D. address the next question you planned to ask to him directly

14. A member of a decision-making conference generally makes his BEST contribution to the conference when he 14.____

   A. compromises on his own point of view and accepts most of the points of other conference members
   B. persuades the conference to accept all or most of his points

C. persuades the conference to accept his major proposals but will yield on the minor ones
D. succeeds in integrating his ideas with the ideas of the other conference members

15. Of the following, the LEAST accurate statement concerning the compilation and use of statistics in administration is:

A. Interpretation of statistics is as necessary as their compilation.
B. Statistical records of expenditures and services are one of the bases for budget preparation.
C. Statistics on the quality of services rendered to the community will clearly delineate the human values achieved.
D. The results achieved from collecting and compiling statistics must be in keeping with the cost and effort required.

16. An important administrative problem is how precisely to define the limits on authority that is delegated to subordinate supervisors.
Such definition of limits of authority SHOULD be

A. as precise as possible and practicable in all areas
B. as precise as possible and practicable in all areas of function, but should allow considerable flexibility in the area of personnel management
C. as precise as possible and practicable in the area of personnel management, but should allow considerable flexibility in the areas of function
D. in general terms so as to allow considerable flexibility both in the areas of function and in the areas of personnel management

17. The LEAST important of the following reasons why a particular activity should be assigned to a unit which performs activities dissimilar to it is that

A. close coordination is needed between the particular activity and other activities performed by the unit
B. it will enhance the reputation and prestige of the unit supervisor
C. the unit makes frequent use of the results of this particular activity
D. the unit supervisor has a sound knowledge and understanding of the particular activity

18. The MOST important of the following reasons why the average resident of a deteriorated slum neighborhood resists relocation to an area in the suburbs with better physical accommodations is that he

A. does not recognize as undesirable the characteristics which are responsible for deterioration of the neighborhood
B. has some expectation of neighborly assistance in his old home in times of stress and adversity
C. hopes for better days when he may be able to become a figure of some importance and envy in the old neighborhood
D. is attuned to the noise of the city and fears the quiet of the suburb

19. From a psychological and sociological point of view, the MOST important of the following dangers to the persons living in an economically depressed area in which the only step taken by governmental and private social agencies to assist these persons is the granting of a dole is that

19.____

    A. industry will be reluctant to expand its operations in that area
    B. the dole will encourage additional non-producers to enter the area
    C. the residents of the area will probably have to find their own solution to their problems
    D. their permanent dependency will be fostered

20. The term *real wages* is GENERALLY used by economists to mean the

20.____

    A. amount of take-home pay left after taxes, social security, and other such deductions have been made by the employer
    B. average wage actually earned during a calendar or fiscal year
    C. family income expressed on a per capita basis
    D. wages expressed in terms of its buyer power

21. It has, at times, been suggested that an effective way to eradicate juvenile delinquency would be to arrest and punish the parents for the criminal actions of their delinquent children.
The one of the following which is the CHIEF defect of this proposal is that

21.____

    A. it fails to get at the cause of the delinquent act and tends to further weaken disturbed parent-child relationships
    B. since the criminally inclined child has apparently demonstrated little love or affection for his parent, the child will be unlikely to amend his behavior in order to avoid hurting his parent
    C. the child who commits anti-social acts does so in many cases in order to hurt his parents so that this proposal would not only increase the parents' sorrow, but would also serve as an incentive to more delinquency by the child
    D. the punishment should be limited to the person who commits the illegal action rather than to those who are most interested in his welfare

22. Surveys which have compared the relative stability of marriages between white persons with marriages between non-white persons in this country have shown that, among Blacks, there is

22.____

    A. a significantly higher percentage of spouses absent from the household than among whites
    B. a significantly higher percentage of spouses absent from the household than among whites living in the South, but the opposite is true in the Northeast
    C. a significantly lower percentage of spouses absent from the household than among whites
    D. no significant difference in the percentage of spouses absent from the household when compared with the white population

23. A phenomenon found in the cultural and recreational patterns of European immigrant families in America is that, generally, the foreign-born adults   23.____

    A. as well as their children, tend soon to forget their old-world activities and adopt the cultural and recreational customs of America

    B. as well as their children, tend to retain and continue their old-world cultural and recreational pursuits, and find it equally difficult to adopt those of America

    C. tend soon to drop their old pursuits and adopt the cultural and recreational patterns of America while their children find it somewhat more difficult to make this change

    D. tend to retain and continue their old-world cultural and recreational pursuits while their children tend to rapidly replace these by the games and cultural patterns of America

24. Certain mores of migrant groups are strengthened under the impact of their contact with the native society while other mores are weakened.   24.____
In the case of Puerto Ricans who have come to the city, the effect of such contact upon their traditional family structure has been a

    A. strengthening of the former maternalistic family structure
    B. strengthening of the former paternalistic family structure
    C. weakening of the former maternalistic family structure
    D. weakening of the former paternalistic family structure

25. Administrative reviews and special studies of independent experts, as reported by the Department of Health, Education and Welfare, indicate that the proportion of recipients of public assistance who receive such assistance through *wilful misrepresentation* of the facts is   25.____

    A. less than 1%   B. about 4%
    C. between 4% and 7%   D. between 7% and 10%

KEY (CORRECT ANSWERS)

1.	B		11.	D
2.	D		12.	A
3.	D		13.	B
4.	B		14.	D
5.	A		15.	C
6.	B		16.	A
7.	D		17.	B
8.	A		18.	B
9.	B		19.	D
10.	C		20.	D

21.	A
22.	A
23.	D
24.	D
25.	A

TEST 2

1. In order to meet more adequately the public assistance needs occasioned by sudden changes in the national economy, social service agencies, in general, recommend, as a matter of preference, that

    1.____

    A. each locality build up reserve funds to care for needy unemployed persons in order to avoid a breakdown of local resources such as occurred during the depression
    B. the federal government assume total responsibility for the administration of public assistance
    C. state settlement laws be strictly enforced so that unemployed workers will be encouraged to move from the emergency industry centers to their former homes
    D. a federal-state-local program of general assistance be established with need as the only eligibility requirement
    E. eligibility requirements be tightened to assure that only legitimately worthy local residents receive the available assistance

2. The MOST practical method of maintaining income for the majority of aged persons who are no longer able to work, or for the families of those workers who are deceased, is a(n)

    2.____

    A. comprehensive system of non-categorical assistance on a basis of cash payments
    B. integrated system of public assistance and extensive work relief programs
    C. co-ordinated system of providing care in institutions and foster homes
    D. system of contributory insurance in which a cash benefit is paid as a matter of right
    E. expanded system of diagnostic and treatment centers

3. With the establishment of insurance and assistance programs under the Social Security Act, many institutional programs for the aged have tended to the greatest extent toward an increased emphasis on providing, of the following types of assistance,

    3.____

    A. care for the aged by denominational groups
    B. care for children requiring institutional treatment
    C. recreational facilities for the able-bodied aged
    D. training facilities in industrial homework for the aged
    E. care for the chronically ill and infirm aged

4. Of the following terms, the one which BEST describes the Social Security Act is

    4.____

    A. enabling legislation
    B. regulatory statute
    C. appropriations act
    D. act of mandamus
    E. provisional enactment

5. Of the following, the term which MOST accurately describes an appropriation is   5.____

    A. authority to spend
    B. itemized estimate
    C. *fund* accounting
    D. anticipated expenditure
    E. executive budget

6. When business expansion causes a demand for labor, the worker group which benefits   6.____
   MOST immediately is the group comprising

    A. employed workers
    B. inexperienced workers under 21 years of age
    C. experienced workers 21 to 25 years of age
    D. inexperienced older workers
    E. experienced workers over 40 years of age

7. The MOST important failure in our present system of providing social work services in   7.____
   local communities is the

    A. absence of adequate facilities for treating mental illness
    B. lack of coordination of available data and service in the community
    C. poor quality of the casework services provided by the public agencies
    D. limitations of the probation and parole services
    E. inadequacy of private family welfare services

8. Recent studies of the relationship between incidence of illness and the use of available   8.____
   treatment services among various population groups in the United States show that

    A. while lower-income families use medical services with greater frequency, total
       expenditures are greater among the upper-income groups
    B. although the average duration of a period of medical care increases with increas-
       ing income, the average frequency of obtaining care decreases with increasing
       income
    C. adequacy of medical service is inversely related to frequency of illness and size of
       family income
    D. families in the higher-income brackets have a heavier incidence of illness and
       make greater use of medical services than do those in the lower-income brackets
    E. both as to frequency and duration, the distribution of illness falls equally on all
       groups, but the use of medical services increases with income

9. The category of disease which most public health departments and authorities usually   9.____
   are NOT equipped to handle *directly* is that of

    A. chronic disease
    B. bronchial disturbances
    C. venereal disease
    D. mosquito-borne diseases
    E. incipient forms of tuberculosis

10. Recent statistical analyses of the causes of death in the United States indicate that med-ical science has now reached the stage where it would be preferable to increase its research toward control, among the following, PRINCIPALLY of   10._____

    A. accidents
    B. suicides
    C. communicable disease
    D. chronic disease
    E. infant mortality

11. Although the distinction between mental disease and mental deficiency is fairly definite, both these conditions USUALLY represent   11._____

    A. diseases of one part or organ of the body rather than of the whole person
    B. an inadequacy existing from birth or shortly afterwards and appearing as a simplic-ity of intelligence
    C. a deficiency developing later in life and characterized by distortions of attitude and belief
    D. inadequacies in meeting life situations and in conducting one's affairs
    E. somewhat transitory conditions characterized by disturbances of consciousness

12. According to studies made by reliable medical research organizations in the United States, differences among the states in proportion of physicians to population are MOST directly related to the   12._____

    A. geographic resources among the states
    B. skill of the physicians
    C. relative proportions of urban and rural people in the population of the states
    D. number of specialists in the ranks of the physicians
    E. health status of the people in the various states

13. One of the MAIN advantages of incorporating a charitable organization is that   13._____

    A. gifts or property of a corporation cannot be held in perpetuity
    B. gifts to unincorporated charitable organizations are not deductible from the taxable income
    C. incorporation gives less legal standing or *personality* than an informal partnership
    D. members of a corporation cannot be held liable for debts contracted by the organi-zation
    E. a corporate organization cannot be sued

14. The BASIC principle underlying a social security program is that the government should provide   14._____

    A. aid to families that is not dependent on state or local participation
    B. assistance to any worthy family unable to maintain itself independently
    C. protection to individuals against some of the social risks that are inherent in an industrialized society
    D. safeguards against those factors leading to economic depression

15. The activities of state and local public welfare agencies are dependent to a large degree   15.____
on the public assistance program of the federal government.
The one of the following which the federal government has NOT been successful in
achieving within the local agencies is the

    A. broadening of the scope of public assistance administration
    B. expansion of the categorical programs
    C. improvement of the quality of service given to clients
    D. standardization of the administration of general assistance programs

16. Of the following statements, the one which BEST describes the federal government's   16.____
position, as stated in the Social Security Act, with regard to tests of character or fitness to
be administered by local or state welfare departments to prospective clients is that

    A. no tests of character are required but they are not specifically prohibited
    B. if tests of character are used, they must be uniform throughout the state
    C. tests of character are contrary to the philosophy of the federal government and are
       to be considered illegal
    D. no tests of character are required, and assistance to those states that use them will
       be withheld

17. An increase in the size of the welfare grant may increase the cost of the welfare program   17.____
not only in terms of those already on the welfare rolls, but because it may result in an
increase in the number of people on the rolls.
The CHIEF reason that an increase in the size of the grant may cause an increase in
the number of people on the rolls is that the increased grant may

    A. induce low-salaried wage earners to apply for assistance rather than continue at
       their menial jobs
    B. make eligible for assistance many people whose resources are just above the pre-
       vious standard
    C. induce many people to apply for assistance who hesitated to do so because of
       meagerness of the previous grant
    D. make relatives less willing to contribute because the welfare grant can more ade-
       quately cover their dependents' needs

18. One of the MAIN differences between the use of casework methods by a public welfare   18.____
agency and by a private welfare agency is that the public welfare agency

    A. requires that the applicant be eligible for the services it offers
    B. cannot maintain a non-judgmental attitude toward its clients because of legal
       requirements
    C. places less emphasis on efforts to change the behavior of its clients
    D. must be more objective in its approach to the client because public funds are
       involved

19. All definitions of social casework include certain major assumptions.   19.____
Of the following, the one which is NOT considered a major assumption is that

    A. the individual and society are interdependent
    B. social forces influence behavior and attitudes, affording opportunity for self-devel-
       opment and contribution to the world in which we live
    C. reconstruction of the total personality and reorganization of the total environment
       are specific goals
    D. the client is a responsible participant at every step in the solution of his problems

20. In order to provide those services to problem families which will help restore them to a   20._____
    self-maintaining status, it is necessary to FIRST

    A. develop specific plans to meet the individual needs of the problem family
    B. reduce the size of those caseloads composed of multi-problem families
    C. remove them from their environment and provide them with the means of overcom-
       ing their dependency
    D. identify the factors causing their dependency and creating problems for them

21. Of the following, the type of service which can provide the client with the MOST enduring   21._____
    help is that service which

    A. provides him with material aid and relieves the stress of his personal problems
    B. assists him to do as much as he can for himself and leaves him free to make his
       own decisions
    C. directs his efforts towards returning to a self-maintaining status and provides him
       with desirable goals
    D. gives him the feeling that the agency is interested in him as an individual and
       stands ready to assist him with his problems

22. Psychiatric interpretation of unconscious motivations can bring childhood conflicts into   22._____
    the framework of adult understanding and open the way for them to be resolved, but the
    interpretation must come from within the client.
    This statement means MOST NEARLY that

    A. treatment is merely diagnosis in reverse
    B. explaining a client to himself will lead to the resolution of his problems
    C. the client must arrive at an understanding of his problems
    D. unresolved childhood conflicts create problems for the adult

23. A significant factor in the United States economic picture is the state of the labor market.   23._____
    Of the following, the MOST important development affecting the labor market has been

    A. an expansion of the national defense effort creating new plant capacity
    B. the general increase in personal income as a result of an increase in overtime pay
       in manufacturing industries
    C. the growth of manufacturing as a result of automation
    D. a demand for a large number of jobs resulting from new job applicants as well as
       from displacement of workers by automation

24. A typical characteristic of the United States population over 65 is that MOST of them   24._____

    A. are independent and capable of self-support
    B. live in their own homes but require various supportive services
    C. live in institutions for the aged
    D. require constant medical attention at home or in an institution

25. The one of the following factors which is MOST important in preventing persons 65 years   25._____
    of age and older from getting employment is the

    A. misconceptions by employers of skills and abilities of senior citizens
    B. lack of skill in modern industrial techniques of persons in this age group
    C. social security laws restricting employment of persons in this age group
    D. unwillingness of persons in this age group to continue supporting themselves

KEY (CORRECT ANSWERS)

1.	D	11.	D	
2.	D	12.	C	
3.	E	13.	D	
4.	A	14.	C	
5.	A	15.	D	
6.	B	16.	A	
7.	B	17.	B	
8.	C	18.	C	
9.	A	19.	C	
10.	D	20.	D	

21. B
22. C
23. D
24. B
25. A

READING COMPREHENSION
UNDERSTANDING AND INTERPRETING WRITTEN MATERIAL
EXAMINATION SECTION
TEST 1

DIRECTIONS: Each question or incomplete statement is followed by several suggested answers or completions. Select the one that BEST answers the question or completes the statement. *PRINT THE LETTER OF THE CORRECT ANSWER IN THE SPACE AT THE RIGHT.*

Questions 1-8.

DIRECTIONS: Questions 1 through 8 are to be answered on the basis of the following statement.

    The child lives in a context which is itself neither simple nor unitary and which continuously affects his behavior and development. Patterns of stimulation come to him out of this context. In turn, by virtue of his own make-up, he selects from that context. At all times, there is a reciprocal relation between the human organism and this biosocial context. Because the child is limited in time, behavior becomes structured, and patterns develop both in the stimulus field and in his own response system. Some stimulus patterns become significant because they modify the developmental stream by affecting practice or social relations with others. Others remain insignificant because they do not affect this web of relations. Why one pattern is significant and another is not is a crucial problem for child psychology.

1.   The author states that   1.____

    A.   environmental forces have an important effect in determining both the child's actions and his course of growth
    B.   environmental and hereditary forces play an equal part in determining both the child's actions and his course of growth
    C.   even the environmental forces which are not consciously important to the child can affect both learning and personality
    D.   the child's personality is shaped more by the total pattern of pressures in the environment

2.   The author develops *context* so as to make it mean   2.____

    A.   the nature of the child's immediate environment
    B.   a complex rather than a simple home structure
    C.   a multitude of past, present, and future forces
    D.   internal as well as external influences

3.   According to the author, the CRITICAL forces to be studied are those which   3.____

    A.   are unconscious forces
    B.   are conscious, unconscious, and subconscious forces
    C.   cause the child to respond
    D.   modify the child's interpersonal relationships

4. The author's point of view might BEST be labeled as 4.____

   A. environmentalist   B. behaviorist
   C. psychobiosocial   D. gestaltist

5. The author maintains that the environment 5.____

   A. is relatively stable
   B. is in a constant state of flux
   C. shows periods of marked instability
   D. is more stable than unstable

6. From the above paragraph, it is to be inferred that the 6.____

   A. child's personality is mechanistically determined by the nature of the environment
   B. unique interaction between the child and his environment shapes his personality
   C. child really shapes his own personality
   D. child's personality is more likely to be affected by than to affect the environment

7. By *structured behavior,* the author means 7.____

   A. conditioning of responses
   B. differentiated activity
   C. characteristic modes of reaction
   D. responses that have been modified by the developmental stream

8. The *patterns* to which the author refers are 8.____

   A. different for all children
   B. culturally determined mainly
   C. biologically determined mainly
   D. psychologically determined mainly

Questions 9-13.

DIRECTIONS: Questions 9 through 13 are to be answered on the basis of the following passage.

The Division of Child Guidance makes certain provisions for summer vacations for children receiving foster care. Foster parents wishing to take the child on a vacation within the United States must file Form CG-42 in duplicate at the office of the Division not later than 3 weeks prior to the starting date of the planned vacation. Such request must be approved in writing by the Social Investigator and the Assistant Supervisor. After the request has been approved, the original copy of Form CG-42 must be returned to the foster parents by the Social Investigator no later than 3 days prior to the planned starting date of the vacation. The city continues to pay the foster parents the standard rate for the child's care.

If the foster parents plan to take the child on a vacation outside the continental United States, Form CG-42 must be submitted in triplicate and must be received no later than 5 weeks prior to the starting date of the planned vacation. Such Form CG-42 for vacation outside the country must also be approved by the Case Supervisor. There will be no payment for time spent outside the United States.

When the approved original Form CG-42 is returned to the foster parents, it shall be accompanied by an original copy of Form CG-43. A duplicate copy of Form CG-43 shall be forwarded by the Case Supervisor to the Children's Accounts Section to stop payment for time expected to be spent outside the United States.

9. When a foster parent plans to take his foster child on a vacation trip, the Division of Child Guidance must receive Form

9.____

   A. CG-42 in triplicate no later than five weeks prior to the scheduled start of his vacation trip to Canada
   B. CG-42 in duplicate no later than three weeks prior to the scheduled start of his vacation trip to Mexico
   C. CG-43 in triplicate no later than three weeks prior to the scheduled start of his vacation trip to Arizona
   D. CG-43 in duplicate no later than five weeks prior to the scheduled start of his vacation trip regardless of location

10. The one of the following steps which is required in processing a request from a foster parent to take a child on a vacation trip is that the

10.____

   A. Case Supervisor send the original copy of Form CG-42 to the appropriate section in the case of a child who will spend all his vacation in a foreign country
   B. Children's Accounts Section receive the duplicate copy of Form CG-43 in the case of a child who will spend any part of his vacation in a foreign country
   C. Division of Child Guidance keep a permanent file of original copies of Form CG-43 to keep a control of all current vacation requests
   D. foster parents receive the triplicate copy of Form CG-42 from the Social Investigator in the case of a child who will spend part of his vacation in the United States

11. When a foster child spends an approved vacation with his foster father, payment for the child's care will be given to the foster father for

11.____

   A. none of the time if part of the vacation is spent in a foreign country
   B. that part of the vacation spent inside the United States but a reduced daily rate
   C. the entire period at a standard rate if the vacation is spent wholly in the United States
   D. the entire time regardless of whether or not it is spent in a foreign country

12. The Division of Child Guidance must notify a foster parent that his request to take his foster child on a vacation outside the country has been approved by sending him the approved _____ copy of Form CG-42 and _____ copy of Form CG-43.

12.____

   A. duplicate; duplicate   B. duplicate; original
   C. original; duplicate   D. original; original

13. On the basis of the above passage, children receiving foster care may be taken on a vacation trip by their foster parents to a location

13.____

   A. anywhere in the world with the written approval of the Social Investigator only
   B. of the foster parents' choosing but only with the written approval of both the Assistant Supervisor and Case Supervisor
   C. outside the United States but only with the written approval of the Social Investigator, Assistant Supervisor, and Case Supervisor
   D. within the United States with the written approval of the Case Supervisor only

Questions 14-18.

DIRECTIONS: Questions 14 through 18 are statements based on the following paragraphs. For each question, there are two statements.

Based on the information in the paragraphs, mark your answer A, B, or C, as follows:
A, if only statement 1 is correct;
B, if only statement 2 is correct;
C, if both statements are correct.
Mark your answer D if the excerpts do not contain sufficient evidence for concluding whether either or both statements are correct.

Almost 49,000 children were living in foster family homes or voluntary institutions in the state at the end of 2003. These were children whose parents or relatives were unable or unwilling to care for them in their own homes. The State Department of Social Services supervised the care of these children served under the auspices of 64 social services districts and more than 150 private agencies and institutions. Almost 8 out of every 1,000 children 18 years of age or younger were in care away from their homes at the end of 2003. This estimate does not include a substantial, but unknown, number of children living outside their own homes who were placed there by their parents, relatives, or others without the assistance of a social agency.

The number of children in care (dependent, neglected, and delinquent combined) was up by 4,500 or 10 percent over the 2000-2003 period. Both the city and state reported similar increases. In the comparable period, the state's child population (18 years or less) rose only three percent. Thus, the foster care rate showed a moderate increase to 7.7 per thousand in 2003 from 7.2 thousand in 2000. The city's foster care rate in 2003, at 10.5 per thousand, was almost twice that for upstate New York, 5.7 per thousand. (Excluding delinquent children from the total in care in the state reduces the foster care rate per thousand to 7.2 in 2003 and the comparable 2000 figure to 6.7.)

Dependent and neglected children made up about 95 percent of the total number in foster family homes and voluntary institutions in the state at the end of 2003, as they did in 2000. Delinquent children sent into care (outside the state training school system) by the Family Court accounted for only 5 percent of the total. The number of delinquent children in care rose 5 percent, as an increase in the state, 28 percent, more than offset a 13 percent decline in the city. Delinquents comprised 4.9 percent of the total number of children in care upstate at the end of 2003 and 3.9 percent in the city.

14.   1. There were 45,000 children in care away from their own homes over the 2000-2003   14._____
          period.
        2. The percentage decline of delinquent children in care in the city in 2003 was offset by
          a greater increase in the rest of the state.

15.   1. The increase in delinquent care rate in the state from 2000 to 2003 cannot be deter-   15._____
          mined from the data given.
        2. The state's foster care rate in 2003, exclusive of the city, was about one-half the rate
          for the city.

16. 1. In 2000 and in 2003, the percentage of dependent and neglected children in foster family homes and voluntary institutions in the state was about the same.
    2. In 2000, the number of dependent and neglected children in foster family homes and voluntary institutions in the state was 43,250.

16.____

17. 1. The city's child population rose approximately three percent from 2000 to 2003.
    2. At the end of 2003, less than 1% of the children 18 years of age or younger were in care.

17.____

18. 1. Delinquents in the city comprised 4.4 percent of the total number of children in care in the city at the end of 2000.
    2. An unsubstantial number of children living outside their own homes were placed by their parents or relatives without the assistance of a social agency.

18.____

Questions 19-25.

DIRECTIONS: Questions 19 through 25 are to be answered SOLELY on the basis of the information contained in the following paragraph. Each question consists of a statement. You are to indicate whether the statement is TRUE (T) or FALSE (F).

RESPONSIBILITY OF PARENTS

In a recent survey, ninety percent of the people interviewed felt that parents should be held responsible for the delinquency of their children. Forty-eight out of fifty states have laws holding parents criminally responsible for contributing to the delinquency of their children. It is generally accepted that parents are a major influence in the early moral development of their children. Yet, in spite of all this evidence, practical experience seems to prove that *punish the parents* laws are wrong. Legally, there is some question about the constitutionality of such laws. How far can one person be held responsible for the actions of another? Further, although there are many such laws, the fact remains that they are rarely used and where they are used, they fail in most cases to accomplish the end for which they were intended.

19. Nine out of ten of those interviewed held that parents should be responsible for the delinquency of their children.

19.____

20. Forty-eight percent of the states have laws holding parents responsible for contributing to the delinquency of their children.

20.____

21. Most people feel that parents have little influence on the early moral development of their children.

21.____

22. Experience seems to indicate that laws holding parents responsible for children's delinquency are wrong.

22.____

23. There is no doubt that laws holding parents responsible for delinquency of their children are within the Constitution.

23.____

24. Laws holding parents responsible for delinquent children are not often enforced.

24.____

25. *Punish the parent* laws usually achieve their purpose.

25.____

KEY (CORRECT ANSWERS)

1.	A		11.	C
2.	D		12.	D
3.	D		13.	C
4.	C		14.	B
5.	B		15.	B
6.	B		16.	A
7.	C		17.	D
8.	A		18.	D
9.	A		19.	T
10.	B		20.	F

21.	F
22.	T
23.	F
24.	T
25.	F

TEST 2

DIRECTIONS: Each question or incomplete statement is followed by several suggested answers or completions. Select the one that BEST answers the question or completes the statement. *PRINT THE LETTER OF THE CORRECT ANSWER IN THE SPACE AT THE RIGHT.*

Questions 1-3.

DIRECTIONS: Questions 1 through 3 are to be answered SOLELY on the basis of the following passage.

Undoubtedly, the ultimate solution to the housing problem of the hard-core slum does not lie in code enforcement, however defined. The only solution to that problem is demolition, clearance, and new construction. However, it is also clear that, even with government assistance, new construction is not keeping pace with the obsolescence and deterioration of the existing housing inventory of our cities. Add to this the facts of an increasing population and the continuing migration into metropolitan areas, as well as the demands for more and better housing that grow out of continuing economic prosperity and high employment, and some intimation may be gained of the dimensions of the problem of maintaining our housing supply so that it may begin to meet the need.

1. The one of the following that would be the MOST appropriate title for the above passage is   1.____

    A. PROBLEMS ASSOCIATED WITH MAINTAINING AN ADEQUATE HOUSING SUPPLY
    B. DEMOLITION AS A REMEDY FOR HOUSING PROBLEMS
    C. GOVERNMENT'S ESSENTIAL ROLE IN CODE ENFORCEMENT
    D. THE ULTIMATE SOLUTION TO THE HARD-CORE SLUM PROBLEM

2. According to the above passage, housing code enforcement is   2.____

    A. a way to encourage local initiative in urban renewal
    B. a valuable tool that has fallen into disuse
    C. inadequate as a solution to slum housing problems
    D. responsible for some of the housing problems since the code has not been adequately defined

3. The above passage makes it clear that the BASIC solution to the housing problem is to   3.____

    A. erect new buildings after demolition and site clearance
    B. discourage migration into the metropolitan area
    C. increase rents paid to landlords
    D. enforce the housing code strictly

Questions 4-5.

DIRECTIONS: Questions 4 and 5 are to be answered SOLELY on the basis of the following passage.

Under common law, the tenant was obliged to continue to pay rent, at the risk of eviction, regardless of the condition of the premises. This obligation was based on the following established common law principles: first, that in the absence of express agreement, a lease does not contain any implied warranty of fitness or habitability; second, that the person in possession of premises has the obligation to repair and maintain them; and third, that a lease conveys an interest in real estate rather than binding one to a mutual obligation. Once having conveyed his property, the landlord's right to rent was unconditional. Thus, even if he made an express agreement to repair, the landlord's right to rent remained independent of his promise to repair. This doctrine, known as the *independence of covenants,* required the tenant to continue to pay rent or risk eviction, and to bring a separate action against the landlord for damages resulting from his breach of agreement to repair.

4. According to the above passage, common law provided that a lease would   4.____

    A. bar an ex parte action
    B. bind the parties thereto to a reciprocal obligation
    C. provide an absolute defense for breach of agreement
    D. transmit an interest in real property

5. According to the above passage, the *independence of covenants* required that the   5.____

    A. tenant continue to pay rent even for unfit housing
    B. landlord hold rents in escrow for aggrieved tenants
    C. landlord show valid cause for non-performance of lease requirements
    D. tenant surrender the demised premises in improved condition

Questions 6-11.

DIRECTIONS: Questions 6 through 11 are to be answered SOLELY on the basis of the information given in the following passage.

The City of X has set up a Maximum Base Rent Program for all rent-controlled apartments. The objective is to insure that the landlord will get a fair, but not excessive, profit on his building to stem the great tide of buildings being abandoned by their owners, and to encourage landlords to continue the upkeep of their property. The Maximum Base Rent Program permits the landlord to raise rents under carefully devised standards, while practically no raises in rents in this City were permitted under previous guidelines.

Under this plan, the City determines a Maximum Base Rent amount by means of a formula which takes into account the age of the building, the number of apartments, total rents received from the building, the amount of expenses, and labor costs. The Maximum Base Rent amount is to be recomputed every two years to allow for increases or decreases in building costs.

The Maximum Base Rent, which will allow the landlord to make a *fair return* on his investment, may not be collected immediately, however, since no rent increases over 7.5 percent will be permitted in any one year. The highest actual rent for each apartment during a given year will be called the Maximum Collectible Rent. This will be computed so that the increase over the present rent is not more than 7.5 percent ($7.50 on every $100.00). Sometimes, it may be less. Therefore, collectible rents will increase each year until the Maximum Base Rent is reached.

6. According to the above passage, the Maximum Base Rent is determined by the   6._____

    A. landlord   B. Mayor
    C. Rent Commissioner   D. City

7. Which of the following, according to the above passage, permits a *fair return* on the land-   7._____
lord's investment?
The _____ Rent Program.

    A. Minimum Base   B. Maximum Base
    C. Minimum Collectible   D. Maximum Collectible

8. It may be concluded from the above passage that the City of X hopes that insuring fair   8._____
profits for landlords will be followed by

    A. good upkeep of apartment buildings
    B. decreased interest rates on home mortgages
    C. lower rents in the future
    D. a better formula for determining rents

9. According to the above passage, guidelines for determining rents previous to the Maxi-   9._____
mum Base Rent Program resulted in

    A. practically no raises in rents being made
    B. rent increases of approximately 10 percent a year
    C. a *fair return* to landlords from most rents
    D. landlords making too much money on their property

10. Based on the above passage, which is the MOST correct description of the kinds of facts   10._____
that are taken into consideration when determining the Maximum Base Rent? Facts
about

    A. labor costs and politics
    B. the landlord and labor costs
    C. the building and labor costs
    D. the building and the landlord

11. According to the above passage, the MAXIMUM annual increase in rent for a tenant in   11._____
rent-controlled housing under the Maximum Base Rent Program is

    A. 7.5 percent each year for ten years
    B. 7.5 percent each year until the Maximum Base Rent is reached
    C. always under 7.5 percent a year
    D. $7.50 each year until it reaches $100.00

Questions 12-15.

DIRECTIONS: Questions 12 through 15 are to be answered SOLELY on the basis of the information contained in the following paragraph.

In all projects (except sites), when the Manager determines that a vacant apartment is to
be permanently removed from the rent roll for any reason, e.g., the apartment has been con-
verted to an office or community space, he shall notify the cashier by memorandum. The
cashier shall enter the reduction in dwelling units in the Rent Control Book as of the first of the

month following the date on which the apartment was vacated. He shall also prepare a reduction in Rent Roll (Form 105.046), the original of which is to be attached to the file copy of the Project Monthly Summary for the month during which the reduction is effective. Copies are to be sent to the Finance and Audit Department, Budget Section, and to the Chief of Insurance.

12. The purpose of the above paragraph is to provide for a procedure in handling   12.____

    A. the accounting for space occupied by offices and community centers
    B. apartments not rented as of the first of the month following the date on which the apartment was vacated
    C. vacant apartments temporarily used as office space
    D. vacant apartments permanently removed from the rent roll

13. The Rent Control Book is a control on the amount of monthly rents charged.   13.____
According to the above paragraph, another function of the Rent Control Book is to indicate the

    A. number of offices and community spaces available in the project
    B. number of dwelling units in the project
    C. number of vacant apartments in the project
    D. rental loss for all offices and community spaces

14. In accordance with the above paragraph, the original of the Form 105.046 is to be   14.____

    A. sent to Central Office with the Project Monthly Summary
    B. kept in the project files with the project copy of the Project Monthly Summary
    C. sent to the Finance and Audit Department
    D. sent to the Chief of Insurance

15. The MOST likely reason for informing the Chief of Insurance of the removal of an apartment from the rent roll is to notify him   15.____

    A. to make adjustments in the insurance coverage
    B. of a future change in the address of the office or community space
    C. of a change in the project rent income
    D. of a possible increase in the number of project employees

Questions 16-20.

DIRECTIONS: Questions 16 through 20 are to be answered SOLELY on the basis of the information provided in the following passage.

It is the Housing Administration's policy that all tenants, whether new or transferring from one housing development to another, should be required to pay a standard security deposit of one month's rent based on the rent at the time of admission. There are, however, certain exceptions to this policy. Employees of the Administration shall not be required to pay a security deposit if they secure an apartment in an Administration development. Where the payment of a full security deposit may present a hardship to a tenant, the development's manager may allow a tenant to move into an apartment upon payment of only part of the security deposit. In such cases, however, the tenant must agree to gradually pay the balance of the deposit. If a tenant transfers from one apartment to another within the same project, the security deposit originally paid by the tenant for his former apartment will be acceptable for his new apartment, even if the rent in the new apartment is greater than the rent in the former one. Finally, tenants who receive public assistance need not pay a security deposit before moving into an apartment if the appropriate agency states, in writing, that it will pay the deposit. However, it is the responsibility of the development's manager to make certain that payment shall be received within one month of the date that the tenant moves into the apartment.

16. According to the above passage, when a tenant transfers from one apartment to another in the same development, the Housing Administration will

    A. accept the tenant's old security deposit as the security deposit for his new apartment regardless of the new apartment's rent
    B. refund the tenant's old security deposit and not require him to pay a new deposit
    C. keep the tenant's old security deposit and require him to pay a new deposit
    D. require the tenant to pay a new security deposit based on the difference between his old rent and his new rent

16.____

17. On the basis of the above passage, it is INCORRECT to state that a tenant who receives public assistance may move into an Administration development if

    A. he pays the appropriate security deposit
    B. the appropriate agency gives a written indication that it will pay the security deposit before the tenant moves in
    C. the appropriate agency states, by telephone, that it will pay the security deposit
    D. the appropriate agency writes the manager to indicate that the security deposit will be paid within one month but not less than two weeks from the date the tenant moves into the apartment

17.____

18. On the basis of the above passage, a tenant who transfers from an apartment in one development to an apartment in a different development will

    A. forfeit his old security deposit and be required to pay another deposit
    B. have his old security deposit refunded and not have to pay a new deposit
    C. pay the difference between his old security deposit and the new one
    D. have to pay a security deposit based on the new apartment's rent

18.____

19. The Housing Administration will NOT require payment of a security deposit if a tenant

    A. is an Administration employee
    B. is receiving public assistance
    C. claims that payment will present a hardship
    D. indicates, in writing, that he will be responsible for any damage done to his apartment

19.____

20. Of the following, the BEST title for the above passage is

    A. SECURITY DEPOSITS - TRANSFERS
    B. SECURITY DEPOSITS - POLICY
    C. EXEMPTIONS AND EXCEPTIONS - SECURITY DEPOSITS
    D. AMOUNTS - SECURITY DEPOSITS

20.____

Questions 21-23.

DIRECTIONS: Questions 21 through 23 are to be answered SOLELY on the basis of the following paragraphs.

In our program, we must continually strive to increase public good will and to maintain that good will which we have already established. It is important to remember in all your public contacts that to a good many people you are the Department. Don't take out any of your personal gripes on the public. When we must appeal to the public for cooperation, that is when any good will we have built up will come in handy. If the public has been given incorrect or incomplete help when seeking information or advice, or have received what they considered poor treatment in dealing with members of the Department, they will not provide a sympathetic audience when we direct our appeals to them.

One of the Department activities in which there is considerable contact with the public is inspection. Any activity in this area poses special problems and makes your personal dealings with the individuals involved very important. You must bear in mind that you are dealing with people who are sensitive to the manner in which they are treated and you should guide yourself accordingly.

Let us consider some of the aspects of the actual inspection of the premises:

APPEARANCE - Your appearance will determine the initial impression made on anyone you deal with. It is often difficult to change a person's first impression, so try to make it a favorable one. Be neat and clean; show that you have taken some trouble to make a good appearance. Your appearance should form a part of a business-like attitude that should govern your inspection of any premises.

APPROACH - Be courteous at all times. When you enter a building, immediately seek out the owner or occupant and ask his permission to inspect the premises. Ask him to accompany you on the inspection if he has the time, and explain to him the reasons why such inspections are made. Try to give him the feeling that this is a cooperative effort and that his part in this effort is appreciated. Do not make your approach on the basis that it is your legal right to inspect the premises; a coercive attitude tends to produce a hostile reaction.

21. Of the following, the BEST title for the subject covered in the above paragraphs is   21.____
    A. GOOD MANNERS   B. PUBLIC RELATIONS
    C. NEATNESS   D. INSPECTIONAL DUTIES

22. According to the above paragraphs, the FIRST impression an inspector makes on the   22.____
    public is that of

    A. sympathy   B. courtesy
    C. cleanliness and dress   D. business attitude

23. According to the above paragraphs, if you want the public to cooperate with you, you   23.____
    must

    A. be available at all times
    B. be sure that any information you give them is correct
    C. make sure that their complaints are justified
    D. be stern in your dealings with landlords

Questions 24-25.

DIRECTIONS: Questions 24 and 25 are to be answered SOLELY on the basis of the following passage.

There is no simple solution for controlling crime and deviant behavior. There is no panacea for anti-social conduct. The sooner society gives up the search for a single control solution, the sooner society will be able to face up to the immensity of the task and the never-ending responsibility of our social structure.

24. Which of the following statements is BEST supported by the above passage?   24._____

A. Although crime causation may be considered singular, crime control is many-faceted.
B. When society faces up to the immensity of the crime problem, it will find a single solution to it.
C. A multi-faceted approach to crime control is better than trying to find a single cause or cure.
D. Our social structure is responsible for a continuing search for a simple solution to anti-social behavior.

25. The crime problem can be solved when   25._____

A. it is realized that no solution exists
B. the problem is specifically identified
C. criminals are punished
D. none of the above

_____

KEY (CORRECT ANSWERS)

1.	A		11.	B
2.	C		12.	D
3.	A		13.	B
4.	D		14.	B
5.	A		15.	A
6.	D		16.	A
7.	B		17.	C
8.	A		18.	D
9.	A		19.	A
10.	C		20.	B

21.	B
22.	C
23.	B
24.	C
25.	D

_____

READING COMPREHENSION
UNDERSTANDING AND INTERPRETING WRITTEN MATERIAL
EXAMINATION SECTION
TEST 1

DIRECTIONS: Each question or incomplete statement is followed by several suggested answers or completions. Select the one that BEST answers the question or completes the statement. *PRINT THE LETTER OF THE CORRECT ANSWER IN THE SPACE AT THE RIGHT.*

Questions 1-3.

DIRECTIONS: Questions 1 through 3 are to be answered SOLELY on the basis of the following paragraph.

Every organization needs a systematic method of checking its operations as a means to increase efficiency and promote economy. Many successful private firms have instituted a system of audits or internal inspections to accomplish these ends. Law enforcement organizations, which have an extremely important service to *sell,* should be no less zealous in developing efficiency and economy in their operations. Periodic, organized, and systematic inspections are one means of promoting the achievement of these objectives. The necessity of an organized inspection system is perhaps greatest in those law enforcement groups which have grown to such a size that the principal officer can no longer personally supervise or be cognizant of every action taken. Smooth and effective operation demands that the head of the organization have at hand some tool with which he can study and enforce general policies and procedures and also direct compliance with day-to-day orders, most of which are put into execution outside his sight and hearing. A good inspection system can serve as that tool.

1. The central thought of the above paragraph is that a system of inspections within a police department

   A. is unnecessary for a department in which the principal officer can personally supervise all official actions taken
   B. should be instituted at the first indication that there is any deterioration in job performance by the force
   C. should be decentralized and administered by first-line supervisory officers
   D. is an important aid to the police administrator in the accomplishment of law enforcement objectives

1.____

2. The MOST accurate of the following statements concerning the need for an organized inspection system in a law enforcement organization is: It is

   A. never needed in an organization of small size where the principal officer can give personal supervision
   B. most needed where the size of the organization prevents direct supervision by the principal officer
   C. more needed in law enforcement organizations than in private firms
   D. especially needed in an organization about to embark upon a needed expansion of services

2.____

3. According to the above paragraph, the head of the police organization utilizes the internal inspection system 　　　　　　　　　　　3.___

    A. as a tool which must be constantly re-examined in the light of changing demands for police service

    B. as an administrative technique to increase efficiency and promote economy

    C. by personally visiting those areas of police operation which are outside his sight and hearing

    D. to augment the control of local commanders over detailed field operations

Questions 4-10.

DIRECTIONS: Questions 4 through 10 are to be answered SOLELY on the basis of the following passage.

Job evaluation and job rating systems are intended to introduce scientific procedures. Any type of approach, when properly used, will give satisfactory results. The Point System, when properly validated by actual use, is more likely to be suitable for general use than the ranking system. In many aspects, the Factor Comparison Plan is a point system tied to money values. Of course, there may be another system that combines the ranking system with the point system, especially during the initial stages of the development of the program. After the program has been in use for some time, the tendency is to drop off the ranking phase and continue the use of the point system.

In the ranking system of rating of jobs, every job within the plant is arranged in some order, either from the one with the simplest qualifications to the one with maximum requirements, or in the reverse order. This system should be preceded by careful job analysis and the writing of accurate job descriptions before the rating process is undertaken. It is possible, of course, to take the jobs as they are found in the business enterprise and use the names as they are without any attempt at standardization, and merely rank them according to the general over-all impression of the raters. Such a procedure is certain to fall short of what may reasonably be expected of job rating. Another procedure that is in reality merely a modification of the simple rating described above is to establish a series of grades or zones and arrange all the jobs in the plant into groups within these grades and zones. The practice in most common use is to arrange all the jobs in the plant according to their requirements by rating them and then to establish the classifications or groups.

The actual ranking of jobs may be done by one individual, several individuals, or a committee. If several individuals are working independently on the task, it will usually be found that, in general, they agree but that their rankings vary in certain details. A conference between the individuals, with each person giving his reasons why he rated one way or another, usually produces agreement. The detailed job descriptions are particularly helpful when there is disagreement among raters as to the rating of certain jobs. It is not only possible but desirable to have workers participate in the construction of the job description and in rating the job.

4. The MAIN theme of this passage is 　　　　　　　　　　　　　　　　　　4.___

    A. the elimination of bias in job rating

    B. the rating of jobs by the ranking system

C. the need for accuracy in allocating points in the point system
D. pitfalls to avoid in selecting key jobs in the Factor Comparison Plan

5. The ranking system of rating jobs consists MAINLY of   5._____

A. attaching a point value to each ratable factor of each job prior to establishing an equitable pay scale
B. arranging every job in the organization in descending order and then following this up with a job analysis of the key jobs
C. preparing accurate job descriptions after a job analysis and then arranging all jobs either in ascending or descending order based on job requirements
D. arbitrarily establishing a hierarchy of job classes and grades and then fitting each job into a specific class and grade based on the opinions of unit supervisors

6. The above passage states that the system of classifying jobs MOST used in an organiza-   6._____
tion is to

A. organize all jobs in the organization in accordance with their requirements and then create categories or clusters of jobs
B. classify all jobs in the organization according to the titles and rank by which they are currently known in the organization
C. establish a pre-arranged series of grades or zones and then fit
D. all jobs into one of the grades or zones
E. determine the salary currently being paid for each job and then rank the jobs in order according to salary

7. According to the above passage, experience has shown that when a group of raters is   7._____
assigned to the job evaluation task and each individual rates independently of the others,
the raters GENERALLY

A. agree with respect to all aspects of their rankings
B. disagree with respect to all or nearly all aspects of the rankings
C. disagree on overall ratings, but agree on specific rating factors
D. agree on overall rankings, but have some variance in some details

8. The above passage states that the use of a detailed job description is of SPECIAL value   8._____
when

A. employees of an organization have participated in the preliminary step involved in actual preparation of the job description
B. labor representatives are not participating in ranking of the jobs
C. an individual rater who is unsure of himself is ranking the jobs
D. a group of raters is having difficulty reaching unanimity with respect to ranking a certain job

9. A comparison of the various rating systems as described in the above passage shows   9._____
that

A. the ranking system is not as appropriate for general use as a properly validated point system
B. the point system is the same as the Factor Comparison Plan except that it places greater emphasis on money

C. no system is capable of combining the point system and the Factor Comparison Plan

D. the point system will be discontinued last when used in combination with the Factor Comparison System

10. The above passage implies that the PRINCIPAL reason for creating job evaluation and rating systems was to help   10._____

A. overcome union opposition to existing salary plans
B. base wage determination on a more objective and orderly foundation
C. eliminate personal bias on the part of the trained scientific job evaluators
D. management determine if it was overpricing the various jobs in the organizational hierarchy

Questions 11-13.

DIRECTIONS: Questions 11 through 13 are to be answered SOLELY on the basis of the following paragraph.

The common sense character of the merit system seems so natural to most Americans that many people wonder why it should ever have been inoperative. After all, the American economic system, the most phenomenal the world has ever known, is also founded on a rugged selective process which emphasizes the personal qualities of capacity, industriousness, and productivity. The criteria may not have always been appropriate and competition has not always been fair, but competition there was, and the responsibilities and the rewards – with exceptions, of course – have gone to those who could measure up in terms of intelligence, knowledge, or perseverance. This has been true not only in the economic area, in the money-making process, but also in achievement in the professions and other walks of life.

11. According to the above paragraph, economic rewards in the United States have   11._____

A. always been based on appropriate, fair criteria
B. only recently been based on a competitive system
C. not gone to people who compete too ruggedly
D. usually gone to those people with intelligence, knowledge, and perseverance

12. According to the above passage, a merit system is   12._____

A. an unfair criterion on which to base rewards
B. unnatural to anyone who is not American
C. based only on common sense
D. based on the same principles as the American economic system

13. According to the above passage, it is MOST accurate to say that   13._____

A. the United States has always had a civil service merit system
B. civil service employees are very rugged
C. the American economic system has always been based on a merit objective
D. competition is unique to the American way of life

Questions 14-15.

DIRECTIONS: Questions 14 and 15 are to be answered SOLELY on the basis of the following paragraph.

In-basket tests are often used to assess managerial potential. The exercise consists of a set of papers that would be likely to be found in the in-basket of an administrator or manager at any given time, and requires the individuals participating in the examination to indicate how they would dispose of each item found in the in-basket. In order to handle the in-basket effectively, they must successfully manage their time, refer and assign some work to subordinates, juggle potentially conflicting appointments and meetings, and arrange for follow-up of problems generated by the items in the in-basket. In other words, the in-basket test is attempting to evaluate the participants' abilities to organize their work, set priorities, delegate, control, and make decisions.

14. According to the above paragraph, to succeed in an in-basket test, an administrator must   14.____

    A. be able to read very quickly
    B. have a great deal of technical knowledge
    C. know when to delegate work
    D. arrange a lot of appointments and meetings

15. According to the above paragraph, all of the following abilities are indications of manage-   15.____
rial potential EXCEPT the ability to

    A. organize and control   B. manage time
    C. write effective reports   D. make appropriate decisions

Questions 16-19.

DIRECTIONS: Questions 16 through 19 are to be answered SOLELY on the basis of the following paragraph.

A personnel researcher has at his disposal various approaches for obtaining information, analyzing it, and arriving at conclusions that have value in predicting and affecting the behavior of people at work. The type of method to be used depends on such factors as the nature of the research problem, the available data, and the attitudes of those people being studied to the various kinds of approaches. While the experimental approach, with its use of control groups, is the most refined type of study, there are others that are often found useful in personnel research. Surveys, in which the researcher obtains facts on a problem from a variety of sources, are employed in research on wages, fringe benefits, and labor relations. Historical studies are used to trace the development of problems in order to understand them better and to isolate possible causative factors. Case studies are generally developed to explore all the details of a particular problem that is representative of other similar problems. A researcher chooses the most appropriate form of study for the problem he is investigating. He should recognize, however, that the experimental method, commonly referred to as the scientific method, if used validly and reliably, gives the most conclusive results.

16. The above paragraph discusses several approaches used to obtain information on par-   16.____
ticular problems. Which of the following may be MOST reasonably concluded from the paragraph?
A(n)

A. historical study cannot determine causative factors
B. survey is often used in research on fringe benefits
C. case study is usually used to explore a problem that is unique and unrelated to other problems
D. experimental study is used when the scientific approach to a problem fails

17. According to the above paragraph, all of the following are factors that may determine the type of approach a researcher uses EXCEPT   17._____

A. the attitudes of people toward being used in control groups
B. the number of available sources
C. his desire to isolate possible causative factors
D. the degree of accuracy he requires

18. The words *scientific method*, as used in the last sentence of the above paragraph, refer to a type of study which, according to the above paragraph   18._____

A. uses a variety of sources
B. traces the development of problems
C. uses control groups
D. analyzes the details of a representative problem

19. Which of the following can be MOST reasonably concluded from the above paragraph? In obtaining and analyzing information on a particular problem, a researcher employs the method which is the   19._____

A. most accurate   B. most suitable
C. least expensive   D. least time-consuming

Questions 20-25.

DIRECTIONS: Questions 20 through 25 are to be answered SOLELY on the basis of the following passage.

The quality of the voice of a worker is an important factor in conveying to clients and co-workers his attitude and, to some degree, his character. The human voice, when not consciously disguised, may reflect a person's mood, temper, and personality. It has been shown in several experiments that certain character traits can be assessed with better than chance accuracy through listening to the voice of an unknown person who cannot be seen.

Since one of the objectives of the worker is to put clients at ease and to present an encouraging and comfortable atmosphere, a harsh, shrill, or loud voice could have a negative effect. A client who displays emotions of anger or resentment would probably be provoked even further by a caustic tone. In a face-to-face situation, an unpleasant voice may be compensated for, to some degree, by a concerned and kind facial expression. However, when one speaks on the telephone, the expression on one's face cannot be seen by the listener. A supervising clerk who wishes to represent himself effectively to clients should try to eliminate as many faults as possible in striving to develop desirable voice qualities.

20. If a worker uses a sarcastic tone while interviewing a resentful client, the client, according to the above passage, would MOST likely

    A. avoid the face-to-face situation
    B. be ashamed of his behavior
    C. become more resentful
    D. be provoked to violence

20._____

21. According to the passage, experiments comparing voice and character traits have demonstrated that

    A. prospects for improving an unpleasant voice through training are better than chance
    B. the voice can be altered to project many different psychological characteristics
    C. the quality of the human voice reveals more about the speaker than his words do
    D. the speaker's voice tells the hearer something about the speaker's personality

21._____

22. Which of the following, according to the above passage, is a person's voice MOST likely to reveal?
His

    A. prejudices   B. intelligence
    C. social awareness   D. temperament

22._____

23. It may be MOST reasonably concluded from the above passage that an interested and sympathetic expression on the face of a worker

    A. may induce a client to feel certain he will receive welfare benefits
    B. will eliminate the need for pleasant vocal qualities in the interviewer
    C. may help to make up for an unpleasant voice in the interviewer
    D. is desirable as the interviewer speaks on the telephone to a client

23._____

24. Of the following, the MOST reasonable implication of the above paragraph is that a worker should, when speaking to a client, control and use his voice to

    A. simulate a feeling of interest in the problems of the client
    B. express his emotions directly and adequately
    C. help produce in the client a sense of comfort and security
    D. reflect his own true personality

24._____

25. It may be concluded from the above passage that the PARTICULAR reason for a worker to pay special attention to modulating her voice when talking on the phone to a client is that, during a telephone conversation,

    A. there is a necessity to compensate for the way in which a telephone distorts the voice
    B. the voice of the worker is a reflection of her mood and character
    C. the client can react only on the basis of the voice and words she hears
    D. the client may have difficulty getting a clear under-standing over the telephone

25._____

KEY (CORRECT ANSWERS)

1.	D		11.	D
2.	B		12.	D
3.	B		13.	C
4.	B		14.	C
5.	C		15.	C
6.	A		16.	B
7.	D		17.	D
8.	D		18.	C
9.	A		19.	B
10.	B		20.	C

21.	D
22.	D
23.	C
24.	C
25.	C

TEST 2

Questions 1-3.

DIRECTIONS: Questions 1 through 3 are to be answered SOLELY on the basis of the following paragraph.

Suppose you are given the job of printing, collating, and stapling 8,000 copies of a ten-
page booklet as soon as possible. You have available one photo-offset machine, a collator
with an automatic stapler, and the personnel to operate these machines. All will be available
for however long the job takes to complete. The photo-offset machine prints 5,000 impressions an hour, and it takes about 15 minutes to set up a plate. The collator, including time for
insertion of pages and stapling, can process about 2,000 booklets an hour. (Answers should
be based on the assumption that there are no breakdowns or delays.)

1. Assuming that all the printing is finished before the collating is started, if the job is given   1.____
   to you late Monday and your section can begin work the next day and is able to devote
   seven hours a day, Monday through Friday, to the job until it is finished, what is the BEST
   estimate of when the job will be finished?

   A. Wednesday afternoon of the same week
   B. Thursday morning of the same week
   C. Friday morning of the same week
   D. Monday morning of the next week

2. An operator suggests to you that instead of completing all the printing and then begin-   2.____
   ning collating and stapling, you first print all the pages for 4,000 booklets, so that they
   can be collated and stapled while the last 4,000 booklets are being printed.
   If you accepted this suggestion, the job would be completed

   A. sooner but would require more man-hours
   B. at the same time using either method
   C. later and would require more man-hours
   D. sooner but there would be more wear and tear on the plates

3. Assume that you have the same assignment and equipment as described above, but   3.____
   16,000 copies of the booklet are needed instead of 8,000.
   If you decided to print 8,000 complete booklets, then collate and staple them while you
   started printing the next 8,000 booklets, which of the following statements would
   MOST accurately describe the relationship between this new method and your original
   method of printing all the booklets at one time, and then collating and stapling them?
   The

   A. job would be completed at the same time regardless of the method used
   B. new method would result in the job's being completed 3 1/2 hours earlier
   C. original method would result in the job's being completed an hour later
   D. new method would result in the job's being completed 1 1/2 hours earlier.

Questions 4-6.

DIRECTIONS: Questions 4 through 6 are to be answered SOLELY on the basis of the following passage.

When using words like company, association, council, committee, and board in place of the full official name, the writer should not capitalize these short forms unless he intends them to invoke the full force of the institution's authority. In legal contracts, in minutes, or in formal correspondence where one is speaking formally and officially on behalf of the company, the term Company is usually capitalized, but in ordinary usage, where it is not essential to load the short form with this significance, capitalization would be excessive. (Example: The company will have many good openings for graduates this June.)

The treatment recommended for short forms of place names is essentially the same as that recommended for short forms of organizational names. In general, we capitalize the full form but not the short form. If Park Avenue is referred to in one sentence, then the *avenue* is sufficient in subsequent references. The same is true with words like building, hotel, station, and airport, which are capitalized when part of a proper name changed (Pan Am Building, Hotel Plaza, Union Station, O'Hare Airport), but are simply lower-cased when replacing these specific names.

4. The above passage states that USUALLY the short forms of names of organizations   4._____

    A. and places should not be capitalized
    B. and places should be capitalized
    C. should not be capitalized, but the short forms of names of places should be capitalized
    D. should be capitalized, but the short forms of names of places should not be capitalized

5. The above passage states that in legal contracts, in minutes, and in formal correspondence, the short forms of names of organizations should   5._____

    A. usually not be capitalized
    B. usually be capitalized
    C. usually not be used
    D. never be used

6. It can be INFERRED from the above passage that decisions regarding when to capitalize certain words   6._____

    A. should be left to the discretion of the writer
    B. should be based on generally accepted rules
    C. depend on the total number of words capitalized
    D. are of minor importance

Questions 7-10.

DIRECTIONS: Questions 7 through 10 are to be answered SOLELY on the basis of the following passage.

Use of the systems and procedures approach to office management is revolutionizing the supervision of office work. This approach views an enterprise as an entity which seeks to fulfill definite objectives. Systems and procedures help to organize repetitive work into a routine, thus reducing the amount of decision making required for its accomplishment. As a result, employees are guided in their efforts and perform only necessary work. Supervisors are relieved of any details of execution and are free to attend to more important work. Establishing work guides which require that identical tasks be performed the same way each time permits standardization of forms, machine operations, work methods, and controls. This approach also reduces the probability of errors. Any error committed is usually discovered quickly because the incorrect work does not meet the requirement of the work guides. Errors are also reduced through work specialization, which allows each employee to become thoroughly proficient in a particular type of work. Such proficiency also tends to improve the morale of the employees.

7. The above passage states that the accuracy of an employee's work is INCREASED by   7.____

    A. using the work specialization approach
    B. employing a probability sample
    C. requiring him to shift at one time into different types of tasks
    D. having his supervisor check each detail of work execution

8. Of the following, which one BEST expresses the main theme of the above passage? The   8.____

    A. advantages and disadvantages of the systems and procedures approach to office management
    B. effectiveness of the systems and procedures approach to office management in developing skills
    C. systems and procedures approach to office management as it relates to office costs
    D. advantages of the systems and procedures approach to office management for supervisors and office workers

9. Work guides are LEAST likely to be used when   9.____

    A. standardized forms are used
    B. a particular office task is distinct and different from all others
    C. identical tasks are to be performed in identical ways
    D. similar work methods are expected from each employee

10. According to the above passage, when an employee makes a work error, it USUALLY   10.____

    A. is quickly corrected by the supervisor
    B. necessitates a change in the work guides
    C. can be detected quickly if work guides are in use
    D. increases the probability of further errors by that employee

Questions 11-12.

DIRECTIONS: Questions 11 and 12 are to be answered SOLELY on the basis of the following passage.

The coordination of the many activities of a large public agency is absolutely essential. Coordination, as an administrative principle, must be distinguished from and is independent of cooperation. Coordination can be of either the horizontal or the vertical type. In large organizations, the objectives of vertical coordination are achieved by the transmission of orders and statements of policy down through the various levels of authority. It is an accepted generalization that the more authoritarian the organization, the more easily may vertical coordination be accomplished. Horizontal coordination is arrived at through staff work, administrative management, and conferences of administrators of equal rank. It is obvious that of the two types of coordination, the vertical kind is more important, for at best horizontal coordination only supplements the coordination effected up and down the line.

11. According to the above passage, the ease with which vertical coordination is achieved in a large agency depends upon

    11.____

    A. the extent to which control is firmly exercised from above
    B. the objectives that have been established for the agency
    C. the importance attached by employees to the orders and statements of policy transmitted through the agency
    D. the cooperation obtained at the various levels of authority

12. According to the above passage,

    12.____

    A. vertical coordination is dependent for its success upon horizontal coordination
    B. one type of coordination may work in opposition to the other
    C. similar methods may be used to achieve both types of coordination
    D. horizontal coordination is at most an addition to vertical coordination

Questions 13-17.

DIRECTIONS: Questions 13 through 17 are to be answered SOLELY on the basis of the following situation.

Assume that you are a newly appointed supervisor in the same unit in which you have been acting as a provisional for some time. You have in your unit the following workers:

WORKER I - He has always been an efficient worker. In a number of his cases, the clients have recently begun to complain that they cannot manage on the departmental budget.

WORKER II - He has been under selective supervision for some time as an experienced, competent worker. He now begins to be late for his supervisory conferences and to stress how much work he has to do.

WORKER III - He has been making considerable improvement in his ability to handle the details of his job. He now tells you, during an individual conference, that he does not need such close supervision and that he wants to operate more independently. He says that Worker II is always available when he needs a little information or help but, in general, he can manage very well by himself.

WORKER IV - He brings you a complex case for decision as to eligibility. Discussion of the case brings out the fact that he has failed to consider all the available resources adequately but has stressed the family's needs to include every extra item in the budget. This is the third case of a similar nature that this worker has brought to you recently. This worker and Worker I work in adjacent territory and are rather friendly.

In the following questions, select the option that describes the method of dealing with these workers that illustrates BEST supervisory practice.

13. With respect to supervision of Worker I, the assistant supervisor should   13.____

    A. discuss with the worker, in an individual conference, any problems that he may be having due to the increase in the cost of living

    B. plan a group conference for the unit around budgeting, as both Workers I and IV seem to be having budgetary difficulties

    C. discuss with Workers I and IV together the meaning of money as acceptance or rejection to the clients

    D. discuss with Worker I the budgetary data in each case in relation to each client's situation

14. With respect to supervision of Worker II, the supervisor should   14.____

    A. move slowly with this worker and give him time to learn that the supervisor's official appointment has not changed his attitudes or methods of supervision

    B. discuss the worker's change of attitude and ask him to analyze the reasons for his change in behavior

    C. take time to show the worker how he is avoiding his responsibility in the supervisor-worker relationship and that he is resisting supervision

    D. hold an evaluatory conference with the worker and show him how he is taking over responsibilities that are not his by providing supervision for Worker III

15. With respect to supervision of Worker III, the supervisor should discuss with this worker   15.____

    A. why he would rather have supervision from Worker II than from the supervisor

    B. the necessity for further improvement before he can go on selective supervision

    C. an analysis of the improvement that has been made and the extent to which the worker is able to handle the total job for which he is responsible

    D. the responsibility of the supervisor to see that clients receive adequate service

16. With respect to supervision of Worker IV, the supervisor should   16.____

    A. show the worker that resources figures are incomplete but that even if they were complete, the family would probably be eligible for assistance

    B. ask the worker why he is so protective of these families since there are three cases so similar

    C. discuss with the worker all three cases at the same time so that the worker may see his own role in the three situations

    D. discuss with the worker the reasons for departmental policies and procedures around budgeting

17. With respect to supervision of Workers I and IV, since these two workers are friends and would seem to be influencing each other, the supervisor should   17.____

    A. hold a joint conference with them both, pointing out how they should clear with the supervisor and not make their own rules together

    B. handle the problems of each separately in individual conferences

    C. separate them by transferring one to another territory or another unit

    D. take up the problem of workers asking help of each other rather than from the supervisor in a group meeting

Questions 18-20.

DIRECTIONS: Questions 18 through 20 are to be answered SOLELY on the basis of the following passage.

One of the key supervisory problems in a large municipal recreation department is that
many leaders are assigned to isolated playgrounds or small centers, where it is difficult to
observe their work regularly. Often their facilities are extremely limited. In such settings, as
well as in larger recreation centers, where many recreation leaders tend to have other jobs as
well, there tends to be a low level of morale and incentive. Still, it is the supervisor's task to
help recreation personnel to develop pride in their work and to maintain a high level of performance. With isolated leaders, the supervisor may give advice or assistance. Leaders may be
assigned to different tasks or settings during the year to maximize their productivity and provide new challenges. When it is clear that leaders are not willing to make a real effort to con-
tribute to the department, the possibility of penalties must be considered, within the scope of
departmental policy and the union contract. However, the supervisor should be constructive,
encourage and assist workers to take a greater interest in their work, be innovative, and try to
raise morale and to improve performance in positive ways.

18.   The one of the following that would be the MOST appropriate title for the above passage   18._____
is

A.   SMALL COMMUNITY CENTERS - PRO AND CON
B.   PLANNING BETTER RECREATION PROGRAMS
C.   THE SUPERVISOR'S TASK IN UPGRADING PERSONNEL PERFORMANCE
D.   THE SUPERVISOR AND THE MUNICIPAL UNION - RIGHTS AND OBLIGATIONS

19.   The above passage makes clear that recreation leadership performance in ALL recre-   19._____
ation playgrounds and centers throughout a large city is

A.   generally above average, with good morale on the part of most recreation leaders
B.   beyond description since no one has ever observed or evaluated recreation leaders
C.   a key test of the personnel department's effort to develop more effective hiring
standards
D.   of mixed quality, with many recreation leaders having poor morale and a low level
of achievement

20.   According to the above passage, the supervisor's role is to   20._____

A.   use disciplinary action as his major tool in upgrading performance
B.   tolerate the lack of effort of individual employees since they are assigned to iso-
lated playgrounds or small centers
C.   employ encouragement, advice, and, when appropriate, disciplinary action to
improve performance
D.   inform the county supervisor whenever malfeasance or idleness is detected

Questions 21-25.

DIRECTIONS: Questions 21 through 25 are to be answered SOLELY on the basis of the following passage.

EMPLOYEE LEAVE REGULATIONS

Peter Smith, as a full-time permanent city employee under the Career and Salary Plan, earns an *annual leave allowance*. This consists of a certain number of days off a year with pay and may be used for vacation, personal business, and for observing religious holidays. As a newly appointed employee, during his first 8 years of city service, he will earn an annual leave allowance of 20 days off a year (an average of 1 2/3 days off a month). After he has finished 8 full years of working for the city, he will begin earning an additional 5 days off a year. His *annual leave allowance*, therefore, will then be 25 days a year and will remain at this amount for seven full years. He will begin earning an additional two days off a year after he has completed a total of 15 years of city employment. Therefore, in his sixteenth year of working for the city, Mr. Smith will be earning 27 days off a year as his *annual leave allowance* (an average of 2 1/4 days off a month).

A sick leave allowance of one day a month is also given to Mr. Smith, but it can be used only in cases of actual illness. When Mr. Smith returns to work after *using sick leave allowance*, he must have a doctor's note if the absence is for a total of more than 3 days, but he may also be required to show a doctor's note for absences of 1, 2, or 3 days.

21. According to the above passage, Mr. Smith's *annual leave allowance* consists of a certain number of days off a year which he   21.____

    A. does not get paid for
    B. gets paid for at time and a half
    C. may use for personal business
    D. may not use for observing religious holidays

22. According to the above passage, after Mr. Smith has been working for the city for 9 years, his *annual leave allowance* will be _____ days a year.   22.____

    A. 20   B. 25   C. 27   D. 37

23. According to the above passage, Mr. Smith will begin earning an average of 2 days off a month as his *annual leave allowance* after he has worked for the city for full years.   23.____

    A. 7   B. 8   C. 15   D. 17

24. According to the above passage, Mr. Smith is given a *sick leave allowance* of   24.____

    A. 1 day every 2 months   B. 1 day per month
    C. 1 2/3 days per month   D. 2 1/4 days a month

25. According to the above passage, when he uses *sick leave allowance*, Mr. Smith may be required to show a doctor's note   25.____

    A. even if his absence is for only 1 day
    B. only if his absence is for more than 2 days
    C. only if his absence is for more than 3 days
    D. only if his absence is for 3 days or more

KEY (CORRECT ANSWERS)

1.	C	11.	A
2.	C	12.	D
3.	D	13.	D
4.	A	14.	A
5.	B	15.	C
6.	B	16.	C
7.	A	17.	B
8.	D	18.	C
9.	B	19.	D
10.	C	20.	C

21.	C
22.	B
23.	C
24.	B
25.	A

———

TEST 3

Questions 1-6.

DIRECTIONS: Questions 1 through 6 are to be answered SOLELY on the basis of the following passage.

A folder is made of a sheet of heavy paper (manila, kraft, pressboard, or red rope stock) that has been folded once so that the back is about one-half inch higher than the front. Folders are larger than the papers they contain in order to protect them. Two standard folder sizes are *letter size* for papers that are 8 1/2" x 11" and *legal cap* for papers that are 8 1/2" x 13".

Folders are cut across the top in two ways: so that the back is straight (straight-cut) or so that the back has a tab that projects above the top of the folder. Such tabs bear captions that identify the contents of each folder. Tabs vary in width and position. The tabs of a set of folders that are *one-half cut* are half the width of the folder and have only two positions.

One-third cut folders have three positions, each tab occupying a third of the width of the folder. Another standard tabbing is *one-fifth cut*, which has five positions. There are also folders with *two-fifths cut*, with the tabs in the third and fourth or fourth and fifth positions.

1. Of the following, the BEST title for the above passage is

   A. FILING FOLDERS
   C. THE USES OF THE FOLDER
   B. STANDARD FOLDER SIZES
   D. THE USE OF TABS

   1.____

2. According to the above passage, one of the standard folder sizes is called

   A. Kraft cut
   C. one-half cut
   B. legal cap
   D. straight-cut

   2.____

3. According to the above passage, tabs are GENERALLY placed along the _____ of the folder.

   A. back
   C. left side
   B. front
   D. right side

   3.____

4. According to the above passage, a tab is GENERALLY used to

   A. distinguish between standard folder sizes
   B. identify the contents of a folder
   C. increase the size of the folder
   D. protect the papers within the folder

   4.____

5. According to the above passage, a folder that is two-fifths cut has _____ tabs.

   A. no   B. two   C. three   D. five

   5.____

6. According to the above passage, one reason for making folders larger than the papers they contain is that

   A. only a certain size folder can be made from heavy paper
   B. they will protect the papers
   C. they will aid in setting up a tab system
   D. the back of the folder must be higher than the front

   6.____

Questions 7-15.

DIRECTIONS: Questions 7 through 15 are to be answered SOLELY on the basis of the following passage.

The City University of New York traces its origins to 1847, when the Free Academy,
which later became City College, was founded as the first tuition-free municipal college. City
and Hunter Colleges were placed under the direction of the Board of Higher Education in
1926, and Brooklyn and Queens Colleges were subsequently added to the system of municipal colleges. In 1955, Staten Island Community College, the first of the two-year colleges
sponsored by the Board of Higher Education under the program of the State University of
New York, joined the system.

In 1961, the four senior colleges and three community colleges then under the jurisdic-
tion of the Board of Higher Education became the City University of New York, and a University Graduate Division was organized to offer programs leading to the Ph.D. Since then, the
university has undergone even more rapid growth. Today, it consists of nine senior colleges,
an upper division college which admits students at the junior level, eight community colleges,
a graduate division, and an affiliated medical center.

In the summer of 1969, the Board of Higher Education resolved that the time had come
to commit the resources of the university to meeting an urgent social need—unrestricted
access to higher education for all youths of the City. Determined to prevent the waste of
human potential represented by the thousands of high school graduates whose limited educational opportunities left them unable to meet existing admission standards, the Board
moved to adopt a policy of Open Admissions. It was their judgment that the best way of determining whether a potential student can benefit from college work is to admit him to college,
provide him with the learning assistance he needs, and then evaluate his performance.

Beginning with the class of June 1970, every New York City resident who received a high
school diploma from a public or private high school was guaranteed a place in one of the colleges of City University.

7.   Of the following, the BEST title for the above passage is   7._____

    A.   A BRIEF HISTORY OF THE CITY UNIVERSITY
    B.   HIGH SCHOOLS AND THE CITY UNIVERSITY
    C.   THE COMPONENTS OF THE UNIVERSITY
    D.   TUITION-FREE COLLEGES

8.   According to the above passage, which one of the following colleges of the City Univer-   8._____
     sity was ORIGINALLY called the Free Academy?

    A.   Brooklyn College   B.   City College
    C.   Hunter College   D.   Queens College

9.   According to the above passage, the system of municipal colleges became the City Uni-   9._____
     versity of New York in

    A.   1926   B.   1955   C.   1961   D.   1969

10. According to the above passage, Staten Island Community College came under the juris-   10.____
diction of the Board of Higher Education

    A. 6 years after a Graduate Division was organized
    B. 8 years before the adoption of the Open Admissions Policy
    C. 29 years after Brooklyn and Queens Colleges
    D. 29 years after City and Hunter Colleges

11. According to the above passage, the Staten Island Community College is   11.____

    A. a graduate division center
    B. a senior college
    C. a two-year college
    D. an upper division college

12. According to the above passage, the TOTAL number of colleges, divisions, and affiliated   12.____
branches of the City University is

    A. 18   B. 19   C. 20   D. 21

13. According to the above passage, the Open Admissions Policy is designed to determine   13.____
whether a potential student will benefit from college by PRIMARILY

    A. discouraging competition for placement in the City University among high school
       students
    B. evaluating his performance after entry into college
    C. lowering admission standards
    D. providing learning assistance before entry into college

14. According to the above passage, the FIRST class to be affected by the Open Admissions   14.____
Policy was the

    A. high school class which graduated in January 1970
    B. City University class which graduated in June 1970
    C. high school class when graduated in June 1970
    D. City University class which graduated in June 1970

15. According to the above passage, one of the reasons that the Board of Higher Education   15.____
initiated the policy of Open Admissions was to

    A. enable high school graduates with a background of limited educational opportuni-
       ties to enter college
    B. expand the growth of the City University so as to increase the number and variety
       of degrees offered
    C. provide a social resource to the qualified youth of the City
    D. revise admission standards to meet the needs of the City

Questions 16-18.

DIRECTIONS: Questions 16 through 18 are to be answered SOLELY on the basis of the following passage.

Hereafter, all probationary students interested in transferring to community college
career programs (associate degrees) from liberal arts programs in senior colleges (bachelor

degrees) will be eligible for such transfers if they have completed no more than three semesters.

For students with averages of 1.5 or above, transfer will be automatic. Those with 1.0 to 1.5 averages can transfer provisionally and will be required to make substantial progress during the first semester in the career program. Once transfer has taken place, only those courses in which passing grades were received will be computed in the community college grade-point average.

No request for transfer will be accepted from probationary students wishing to enter the liberal arts programs at the community college.

16. According to this passage, the one of the following which is the BEST statement concerning the transfer of probationary students is that a probationary student   16._____

    A. may transfer to a career program at the end of one semester
    B. must complete three semester hours before he is eligible for transfer
    C. is not eligible to transfer to a career program
    D. is eligible to transfer to a liberal arts program

17. Which of the following is the BEST statement of academic evaluation for transfer purposes in the case of probationary students?   17._____

    A. No probationary student with an average under 1.5 may transfer.
    B. A probationary student with an average of 1.3 may not transfer.
    C. A probationary student with an average of 1.6 may transfer.
    D. A probationary student with an average of .8 may transfer on a provisional basis.

18. It is MOST likely that, of the following, the next degree sought by one who already holds the Associate in Science degree would be a(n)   18._____

    A. Assistantship in Science degree
    B. Associate in Applied Science degree
    C. Bachelor of Science degree
    D. Doctor of Philosophy degree

Questions 19-20.

DIRECTIONS: Questions 19 and 20 are to be answered SOLELY on the basis of the following passage.

Auto: Auto travel requires prior approval by the President and/or appropriate Dean and must be indicated in the *Request for Travel Authorization* form. Employees authorized to use personal autos on official College business will be reimbursed at the rate of 28¢ per mile for the first 500 miles driven and 18¢ per mile for mileage driven in excess of 500 miles. The Comptroller's Office may limit the amount of reimbursement to the expenditure that would have been made if a less expensive mode of transportation (railroad, airplane, bus, etc.) had been utilized. If this occurs, the traveler will have to pick up the excess expenditure as a personal expense.

Tolls, Parking Fees, and Parking Meter Fees are not reimbursable and may not be claimed.

19. Suppose that Professor T. gives the office assistant the following memorandum: 19.____
Used car for official trip to Albany, New York, and return. Distance from New York to
Albany is 148 miles. Tolls were $3.50 each way. Parking garage cost $3.00.
When preparing the Travel Expense Voucher for Professor T., the figure which should
be claimed for transportation is

    A. $120.88   B. $113.88   C. $82.88   D. $51.44

20. Suppose that Professor V. gives the office assistant the following memorandum: 20.____
Used car for official trip to Pittsburgh, Pennsylvania, and return.
Distance from New York to Pittsburgh is 350 miles. Tolls were $3.30, $11.40 going, and
$3.30, $2.00 returning.
When preparing the Travel Expense Voucher for Professor V., the figure which should
be claimed for transportation is

    A. $225.40   B. $176.00   C. $127.40   D. $98.00

Questions 21-25.

DIRECTIONS: Questions 21 through 25 are to be answered SOLELY on the basis of the following passage.

For a period of nearly fifteen years, beginning in the mid-1950's, higher education sustained a phenomenal rate of growth. The factors principally responsible were continuing
improvement in the rate of college entrance by high school graduates, a 50 percent increase
in the size of the college-age (eighteen to twenty-one) group, and – until about 1967 – a rapid
expansion of university research activity supported by the Federal government.

Today, as one looks ahead to the year 2010, it is apparent that each of these favorable
stimuli will either be abated or turn into a negative factor. The rate of growth of the college-
age group has already diminished; and from 2000 to 2005, the size of the college-age group
has shrunk annually almost as fast as it grew from 1965 to 1970. From 2005 to 2010, this
annual decrease will slow down so that by 2010 the age group will be about the same size as
it was in 2009. This substantial net decrease in the size of the college-age group (from 1995
to 2010) will dramatically affect college enrollments since, currently, 83 percent of undergraduates are twenty-one and under, and another 11 percent are twenty-two to twenty-four.

21. Which one of the following factors is NOT mentioned in the above passage as contribut-   21.____
ing to the high rate of growth of higher education?

    A.   A large increase in the size of the eighteen to twenty-one age group
    B.   The equalization of educational opportunities among socio-economic groups
    C.   The Federal budget impact on research and development spending in the higher
        education sector
    D.   The increasing rate at which high school graduates enter college

22. Based on the information in the above passage, the size of the college-age group in   22.____
2010 will be

    A.   larger than it was in 2009
    B.   larger than it was in 1995
    C.   smaller than it was in 2005
    D.   about the same as it was in 2000

23. According to the above passage, the tremendous rate of growth of higher education started around   23._____

    A. 1950   B. 1955   C. 1960   D. 1965

24. The percentage of undergraduates who are over age 24 is MOST NEARLY   24._____

    A. 6%   B. 8%   C. 11%   D. 17%

25. Which one of the following conclusions can be substantiated by the information given in the above passage?   25._____

    A. The college-age group was about the same size in 2000 as it was in 1965.
    B. The annual decrease in the size of the college-age group from 2000 to 2005 is about the same as the annual increase from 1965 to 1970.
    C. The overall decrease in the size of the college-age group from 2000 to 2005 will be followed by an overall increase in its size from 2005 to 2010.
    D. The size of the college-age group is decreasing at a fairly constant rate from 1995 to 2010.

KEY (CORRECT ANSWERS)

1. A		11. C	
2. B		12. C	
3. A		13. B	
4. B		14. C	
5. B		15. A	
6. B		16. A	
7. A		17. C	
8. B		18. C	
9. C		19. C	
10. D		20. B	

21. B
22. C
23. B
24. A
25. B

EXAMINATION SECTION
TEST 1

DIRECTIONS: Each question or incomplete statement is followed by several suggested answers or completions. Select the one that BEST answers the question or completes the statement. *PRINT THE LETTER OF THE CORRECT ANSWER IN THE SPACE AT THE RIGHT.*

1. Of the following methods of conducting an interview, the BEST is to   1.____

   A. ask questions with *yes* or *no* answers
   B. listen carefully and ask only questions that are pertinent
   C. fire questions at the interviewee so that he must answer sincerely and briefly
   D. read standardized questions to the person being interviewed

2. An interviewer should begin with topics which are easy to talk about and which are not threatening.   2.____
    This procedure is useful MAINLY because it

   A. allows the applicant a little time to get accustomed to the situation and leads to freer communication
   B. distracts the attention of the person being interviewed from the main purpose of the questioning
   C. is the best way for the interviewer to show that he is relaxed and confident on the job
   D. causes the interviewee to feel that the interviewer is apportioning valuable questioning time

3. The initial interview will normally be more of a problem to the interviewer than any subsequent interviews he may have with the same person because   3.____

   A. the interviewee is likely to be hostile
   B. there is too much to be accomplished in one session
   C. he has less information about the client than he will have later
   D. some information may be forgotten when later making record of this first interview

4. Most successful interviews are those in which the interviewer shows a genuine interest in the person he is questioning.   4.____
    This attitude would MOST likely cause the individual being interviewed to

   A. feel that the interviewer already knows all the facts in his case
   B. act more naturally and reveal more of his true feelings
   C. request that the interviewer give more attention to his problems, not his personality
   D. react defensively, suppress his negative feelings, and conceal the real facts in his case

5. Questions worded so that the person being interviewed has some hint of the desired answer can modify the person's response.   5.____
    The result of the inclusion of such questions in an interview, even when they are used inadvertently, is to

A. have no effect on the basic content of the information given by the person inter-
    viewed
B. have value in convincing the person that the suggested plan is the best for him
C. cause the person to give more meaningful information
D. reduce the validity of the information obtained from the person

6. The person MOST likely to be a good interviewer is one who   6._____

A. A. is able to outguess the person being interviewed
B. tries to change the attitudes of the persons he interviews
C. controls the interview by skillfully dominating the conversation
D. is able to imagine himself in the position of the person being interviewed

7. The *halo effect* is an overall impression on the interviewer, whether favorable or unfavor-   7._____
    able, usually created by a single trait. This impression then influences the appraisal of all
    other factors.
    A *halo effect* is LEAST likely to be created at an interview where the interviewee is a

A. person of average appearance and ability
B. rough-looking man who uses abusive language
C. young attractive woman being interviewed by a man
D. person who demonstrates an exceptional ability to remember facts

8. Of the following, the BEST way for an interviewer to calm a person who seems to have   8._____
    become emotionally upset as a result of a question asked is for the interviewer to

A. talk to the person about other things for a short time
B. ask that the person control himself
C. probe for the cause of his emotional upset
D. finish the questioning as quickly as possible

9. Of the following, the BEST reason for discarding an ink cartridge is that   9._____

A. the print quality is too dark
B. the print quality is faded
C. the short edge of the sheet is curled
D. the finish on the sheet is smooth and shiny

10. Persons whose native language is not English sometimes experience difficulty in com-   10._____
    munication when visiting public offices.
    The MOST common method used by such persons to overcome the difficulty in com-
    munication is to

A. write in their own language whatever they wish to say
B. hire a professional interpreter
C. ask a patrolman for assistance
D. bring with them an English-speaking friend or relative

Questions 11-20.

DIRECTIONS: In each Question 11 through 20, there is a statement which contains a word
(one of those underlined) that is either incorrectly used because it is not in
keeping with the meaning the quotation is evidently intended to convey, or is
misspelled. There is only one incorrect word in each statement. Of the four
underlined words in each question, determine if the first one should be
replaced by the word lettered A, the second replaced by the word lettered B,
the third replaced by the word lettered C, or the fourth replaced by the word lettered D. Indicate in the space at the right the replacement word you have
selected..

11.   Whether one depends on <u>flourescent</u> or artificial light or both, adequate <u>standards</u>   11.____
should be <u>maintained</u> by means of <u>systematic</u> tests.

    A.   natural   B.   safeguards
    C.   established   D.   routine

12.   A policeman has to be <u>prepared</u> to assume his <u>knowledge</u> as a social <u>scientist</u> in the   12.____
<u>community</u>.

    A.   forced   B.   role
    C.   philosopher   D.   street

13.   It is <u>practically</u> impossible to <u>tell</u> whether a sentence is very long simply by <u>measuring</u> its   13.____
length.

    A.   almost   B.   mark   C.   too   D.   denoting

14.   By <u>using</u> carbon paper, the typist <u>easily</u> is able to <u>insert</u> as many as six <u>copies</u> of a   14.____
report.

    A.   adding   B.   seldom   C.   make   D.   forms

15.   Although all people have many <u>traits</u> in common, a receptionist in her <u>agreements</u> with   15.____
people <u>learns</u> quickly how <u>different</u> each person is from every other person.

    A.   impressions   B.   associations
    C.   decides   D.   various

16.   Strong <u>leaders</u> are <u>required</u> to organize a community for delinquency prevention and for   16.____
<u>dissemination</u> of organized crime and drug addiction.

    A.   tactics   B.   important
    C.   control   D.   meetings

17.   The <u>demonstrators</u>, who were taken to the Criminal Courts building in <u>Manhattan</u>   17.____
(because it was large enough to <u>accommodate</u> them), contended that the arrests were
<u>unwarrented</u>.

    A.   demonstraters   B.   Manhatten
    C.   accomodate   D.   unwarranted

18.   When two or more forms for spelling a word exist, it is <u>advisable</u> to use the <u>preferred</u>   18.____
spelling indicated in the <u>dictionary</u>, and to use it <u>consistantly</u>.

    A.   adviseable   B.   prefered
    C.   dictionery   D.   consistently

19. If you know the language of the <u>foreign</u> country you are visiting, your <u>embarassment</u> will   19.____
    <u>disappear</u> and you will learn a lot more about the customs and <u>characteristics</u> of the
    common people.

    A. foriegn   B. embarrassment
    C. dissappear   D. charactaristics

20. Material consisting of government bulletins, <u>adverticements</u>, <u>catalogues,</u> announce-   20.____
    ments of address changes, and any other <u>periodical</u> material of this nature may be filed
    <u>alphabetically</u> according to subject.

    A. advertisements   B. cataloges
    C. periodicle   D. alphabeticly

Questions 21-24.

DIRECTIONS: Each of the two sentences in Questions 21 through 24 may be correct or may
contain errors in punctuation, capitalization, or grammar.
If there is an error in only Sentence I, mark your answer A.
If there is an error in only Sentence II, mark your answer B.
If there is an error in both Sentence I and Sentence II, mark your answer C.
If both Sentence I and Sentence II are correct, mark your answer D.

21.   I. It is very annoying to have a pencil sharpener, which is not in proper working   21.____
            order.
    II. The building watchman checked the door of Charlie's office and found that
            the lock has been jammed.

22.   I. Since he went on the City Council a year ago, one of his primary concerns   22.____
            has been safety in the streets.
    II. After waiting in the doorway for about 15 minutes, a black sedan appeared.

23.   I. When you are studying a good textbook is important.   23.____
    II. He said he would divide the money equally between you and me.

24.   I. The question is, "How can a large number of envelopes be sealed rapidly   24.____
            without the use of a sealing machine?"
    II. The administrator assigned two stenographers, Mary and I, to the new
            bureau.

Questions 25-26.

DIRECTIONS: In each of Questions 25 and 26, the four sentences are from a paragraph in a
report. They are not in the right order. Which of the following arrangements is
the BEST one?

25.   I. An executive may answer a letter by writing his reply on the face of the letter   25.____
            itself instead of having a return letter typed.
    II. This procedure is efficient because it saves the executive's time, the typist's
            time, and saves office file space.
    III. Copying machines are used in small offices as well as large offices to save
            time and money in making brief replies to business letters.
    IV. A copy is made on a copying machine to go into the company files, while the
            original is mailed back to the sender.

The CORRECT answer is:

A. I, II, IV, III   B. I, IV, II, III
C. III, I, IV, II   D. III, IV,II,I

26.   I. Most organizations favor one of the types but always include the others to a lesser degree.
      II. However, we can detect a definite trend toward greater use of symbolic control.
      III. We suggest that our local police agencies are today primarily utilizing material control.
      IV. Control can be classified into three types: physical, material, and symbolic.

   The CORRECT answer is:

A. IV, II, III, I   B. II, I, IV, III
C. III, IV, II, I   D. IV, I, III, II

26.____

27. Of the following, the MOST effective report writing style is usually characterized by

A. covering all the main ideas in the same paragraph
B. presenting each significant point in a new paragraph
C. placing the least important points before the most important points
D. giving all points equal emphasis throughout the report

27.____

28. Of the following, which factor is COMMON to all types of reports?

A. Presentation of information
B. Interpretation of findings
C. Chronological ordering of the information
D. Presentation of conclusions and recommendations

28.____

29. When writing a report, the one of the following which you should do FIRST is

A. set up a logical work schedule
B. determine your objectives in writing the report
C. select your statistical material
D. obtain the necessary data from the files

29.____

30. Generally,the frequency with which reports are to be submitted or the length of the interval which they cover should depend MAINLY on the

A. amount of time needed to prepare the reports
B. degree of comprehensiveness required in the reports
C. availability of the data to be included in the reports
D. extent of the variations in the data with the passage of time

30.____

31. The objectiveness of a report is its unbiased presentation of the facts.
If this is so, which of the following reports listed below is likely to be the MOST objective?

A. The Best Use of an Electronic Computer in Department Z
B. The Case for Raising the Salaries of Employees in Department A
C. Quarterly Summary of Production in the Duplicating Unit of Department Y
D. Recommendation to Terminate Employee X's Services Because of Misconduct

31.____

Questions 32-37.

DIRECTIONS: Questions 32 through 37 are to be answered only on the basis of the information contained in the charts below which relate to the budget allocations of City
X, a small suburban community. The charts depict the annual budget allocations by department and by expenditures over a five-year period

CITY X BUDGET IN MILLIONS OF DOLLARS

TABLE I. Budget Allocations By Department

Department	1997	1998	1999	2000	2001
Public Safety	30	45	50	40	50
Health and Welfare	50	75	90	60	70
Engineering	5	8	10	5	8
Human Resources	10	12	20	10	22
Conservation and Environment	10	15	20	20	15
Education and Development	15	25	35	15	15
TOTAL BUDGET	120	180	225	150	180

TABLE II. Budget Allocations by Expenditures

Category	1997	1998	1999	2000	2001
Raw Materials and Machinery	36	63	68	30	98
Capital Outlay	12	27	56	15	18
Personal Services	72	90	101	105	64
TOTAL BUDGET	120	180	225	150	160

32. The year in which the SMALLEST percentage of the total annual budget was allocated to   32.____
the Department of Education and Development is

    A. 1997   B. 1998   C. 2000   D. 2001

33. Assume that in 2000 the Department of Conservation and Environment divided its   33.____
annual budget into the three categories of expenditures and in exactly the same proportion as the budget shown in Table II for the year 2000. The amount allocated for capital outlay in the Department of Conservation and Environment's 2000 budget was MOST
NEARLY _____ million.

    A. $2   B. $4   C. $6   D. $10

34. From the year 1998 to the year 2000, the sum of the annual budgets for the Departments   34.____
of Public Safety and Engineering showed an overall _____ of _____ million.

    A. decline; $8   B. increase; $7
    C. decline; $15   D. increase; $22

35. The LARGEST dollar increase in departmental budget allocations from one year to the   35.____
next was in

    A. Public Safety from 1997 to 1998
    B. Health and Welfare from 1997 to 1998
    C. Education and Development from 1999 to 2000
    D. Human Resources from 1999 to 2000

36. During the five-year period, the annual budget of the Department of Human Resources   36.____
was GREATER than the annual budget for the Department of Conservation and Environment in _____ of the years.

   A. none   B. one   C. two   D. three

37. If the total City X budget increases at the same rate from 2001 to 2002 as it did from   37.____
2000 to 2001, the total City X budget for 2002 will be MOST NEARLY _____ million.

   A. $180   B. $200   C. $210   D. $215

Questions 38-44.

DIRECTIONS: Questions 38 through 44 are to be answered ONLY on the basis of the information contained in the graph below, which relates to the work of a public
agency.

No. of work
units completed

Units of each type of work completed by a public agency from 1996
to 2001

Letters written	———————————	Applications Processed	——o——o——
Documents filed	—x——x——x—	Inspections Made	ooooooooooooooooo

38. The year for which the number of units of one type of work completed was less than it   38.____
was for the previous year while the number of each of the other types of work completed
was more than it was for the previous year was

   A. 1997   B. 1998   C. 1999   D. 2000

39. The number of letters written exceeded the number of applications processed by the   39.____
same amount in _____ of the years.

   A. two   B. three   C. four   D. five

40. The year in which the number of each type of work completed was GREATER than the preceding year was   40.____

    A. 1998   B. 1999   C. 2000   D. 2001

41. The number of applications processed and the number of documents filed were the same in   41.____

    A. 1997   B. 1998   C. 1999   D. 2000

42. The total number of units of work completed by the agency   42.____

    A. increased in each year after 1996
    B. decreased from the prior year in two of the years after 1996
    C. was the same in two successive years from 1996 to 2001
    D. was less in 1996 than in any of the following years

43. For the year in which the number of letters written was twice as high as it was in 1996, the number of documents filed was   43.____

    A. the same as it was in 1996
    B. two-thirds of what it was in 1996
    C. five-sixths of what it was in 1996
    D. one and one-half times what it was in 1996

44. The variable which was the MOST stable during the period 1996 through 2001 was   44.____

    A. Inspections Made   B. Letters Written
    C. Documents Filed   D. Applications Processed

Questions 45-50.

DIRECTIONS: Questions 45 through 50 are to be answered ONLY on the basis of the information in the following passage.

    Job evaluation and job rating systems are intended to introduce scientific procedures. Any type of approach, when properly used, will give satisfactory results. The Point System, when properly validated by actual use, is more likely to be suitable for general use than the ranking system. In many aspects, the Factor Comparison Plan is a point system tied to money values. Of course, there may be another system that combines the ranking system with the point system, especially during the initial stages of the development of the program. After the program has been in use for some time, the tendency is to drop off the ranking phase and continue the use of the point system.

    In the ranking system of rating of jobs, every job within the plant is arranged in some order, either from the one with the simplest qualifications to the one with maximum requirements, or in the reverse order. This system should be preceded by careful job analysis and the writing of accurate job descriptions before the rating process is undertaken. It is possible, of course, to take the jobs as they are found in the business enterprise and use the names as they are without any attempt at standardization, and merely rank them according to the general overall impression of the raters. Such a procedure is certain to fall short of what may reasonably be expected of job rating. Another procedure that is in reality merely a modification of the simple rating described above is to establish a series of grades or zones and arrange all the jobs in the plant into groups within these grades and zones. The practice in most common use is to arrange all the jobs in the plant according to their requirements by rating them and then to establish the classifications or groups.

The actual ranking of jobs may be done by one individual, several individuals, or a committee. If several individuals are working independently on the task, it will usually be found that, in general, they agree but that their rankings vary in certain details. A conference between the individuals, with each person giving his reasons why he rated one way or another, usually produces agreement. The detailed job descriptions are particularly helpful when there is disagreement among raters as to the rating of certain jobs. It is not only possible but desirable to have workers participate in the construction of the job description and in rating the job.

45. The MAIN theme of this passage is   45.____

    A. the elimination of bias in job rating
    B. the rating of jobs by the ranking system
    C. the need for accuracy in allocating points in the point system
    D. pitfalls to avoid in selecting key jobs in the Factor Comparison Plan

46. The ranking system of rating jobs consists MAINLY of   46.____

    A. attaching a point value to each ratable factor of each job prior to establishing an equitable pay scale
    B. arranging every job in the organization in descending order and then following this up with a job analysis of the key jobs
    C. preparing accurate job descriptions after a job analysis and then arranging all jobs either in ascending or descending order based on job requirements
    D. arbitrarily establishing a hierarchy of job classes and grades and then fitting each job into a specific class and grade based on the opinions of unit supervisors

47. The above passage states that the system of classifying jobs MOST used in an organi-   47.____
zation is to

    A. organize all jobs in the organization in accordance with their requirements and then create categories or clusters of jobs
    B. classify all jobs in the organization according to the titles and rank by which they are currently known in the organization
    C. establish a pre-arranged series of grades or zones and then fit all jobs into one of the grades or zones
    D. determine the salary currently being paid for each job and then rank the jobs in order according to salary

48. According to the above passage, experience has shown that when a group of raters is   48.____
assigned to the job evaluation task and each individual rates independently of the others,
the raters GENERALLY

    A. agree with respect to all aspects of their rankings
    B. disagree with respect to all or nearly all aspects of the rankings
    C. disagree on overall ratings but agree on specific rating factors
    D. agree on overall ratings but have some variance in some details

49. The above paragraphs state that the use of a detailed job description is of special value   49.____
when

   A. employees of an organization have participated in the preliminary steps involved in actual preparation of the job description
   B. labor representatives are not participating in ranking of the jobs
   C. an individual rater who is unsure of himself is ranking the jobs
   D. a group of raters is having difficulty reaching unanimity with respect to ranking a certain job

50. A comparison of the various rating systems, as described in the above passage, shows   50.____
that

   A. the ranking system is not as appropriate for general use as a properly validated point system
   B. the point system is the same as the Factor Comparison Plan except that it places greater emphasis on money
   C. no system is capable of combining the point system and the Factor Comparison Plan
   D. the point system will be discontinued last when used in connection with the Factor Comparison Plan

---

KEY (CORRECT ANSWERS)

1.	B	11.	A	21.	C	31.	C	41.	C
2.	A	12.	B	22.	C	32.	D	42.	C
3.	C	13.	C	23.	A	33.	A	43.	B
4.	B	14.	C	24.	B	34.	A	44.	D
5.	D	15.	B	25.	C	35.	B	45.	B
6.	D	16.	C	26.	D	36.	B	46.	C
7.	A	17.	D	27.	B	37.	D	47.	A
8.	A	18.	D	28.	A	38.	B	48.	D
9.	B	19.	B	29.	B	39.	B	49.	D
10.	D	20.	A	30.	D	40.	D	50.	A

PREPARING WRITTEN MATERIALS

EXAMINATION SECTION
TEST 1

DIRECTIONS: Each question contains a sentence. Read each sentence carefully to decide whether it is correct. Then, in the space at the right, mark your answer:
- A. If the sentence is incorrect because of bad grammar or sentence structure;
- B. If the sentence is incorrect because of bad punctuation;
- C. If the sentence is incorrect because of bad capitalization;
- D. If the sentence is correct.

Each incorrect sentence has only one type of error. Consider a sentence correct if it has no errors, although there may be other correct ways of saying the same thing.

SAMPLE QUESTION I; One of our clerks were promoted yesterday.

The subject of this sentence is *one,* so the verb should be *was promoted* instead of *were promoted.* Since the sentence is incorrect because of bad grammar, the answer to Sample Question I is A.

SAMPLE QUESTION II: Between you and me, I would prefer not going there.

Since this sentence is correct, the answer to Sample Question II is D.

1. The National alliance of Businessmen is trying to persuade private businesses to hire youth in the summertime.   1._____

2. The supervisor who is on vacation, is in charge of processing vouchers.   2._____

3. The activity of the committee at its conferences is always stimulating.   3._____

4. After checking the addresses again, the letters went to the mailroom.   4._____

5. The director, as well as the employees, are interested in sharing the dividends.   5._____

6. The experiments conducted by professor Alford were described at a recent meeting of our organization.   6._____

7. I shall be glad to discuss these matters with whoever represents the Municipal Credit Union.   7._____

8. In my opinion, neither Mr. Price nor Mr. Roth knows how to operate this office appliance.   8._____

9. The supervisor, as well as the other stenographers, were unable to transcribe Miss Johnson's shorthand notes.   9._____

10. Important functions such as, recruiting and training, are performed by our unit.   10._____

11. Realizing that many students are interested in this position, we sent announcements to all the High Schools.   11.____

12. After pointing out certain incorrect conclusions, the report was revised by Mr. Clark and submitted to Mr. Batson.   12.____

13. The employer contributed two hundred dollars; the employees, one hundred dollars.   13.____

14. He realized that the time, when a supervisor could hire and fire, was over.   14.____

15. The complaints received by Commissioner Regan was the cause of the change in policy.   15.____

16. Any report, that is to be sent to the Federal Security Administration, must be approved and signed by Mr. Yound.   16.____

17. Of the two stenographers, Miss Rand is the more accurate.   17.____

18. Since the golf courses are crowded during the Summer, more men are needed to maintain the courses in good playing condition.   18.____

19. Although he invited Mr. Frankel and I to attend a meeting of the Civil Service Assembly, we were unable to accept his invitation.   19.____

20. Only the employees who worked overtime last week may leave one hour earlier today.   20.____

21. We need someone who can speak french fluently.   21.____

22. A tall, elderly, man entered the office and asked to see Mr. Brown.   22.____

23. The clerk insisted that he had filed the correspondence in the proper cabinet.   23.____

24. "Will you assist us," he asked?   24.____

25. According to the information contained in the report, a large quantity of paper and envelopes were used by this bureau last year.   25.____

KEY (CORRECT ANSWERS)

1.	C		11.	C
2.	B		12.	A
3.	D		13.	D
4.	A		14.	B
5.	A		15.	A
6.	C		16.	B
7.	D		17.	D
8.	D		18.	C
9.	A		19.	A
10.	B		20.	D

21.	C
22.	B
23.	D
24.	B
25.	A

TEST 2

DIRECTIONS: Each question consists of a sentence which may be classified appropriately under one of the following four categories:
- A. Incorrect because of faulty grammar or sentence structure;
- B. Incorrect because of faulty punctuation;
- C. Incorrect because of faulty capitalization;
- D. Correct

Examine each sentence carefully. Then, in the space at the right, print the capital letter preceding the option which is the BEST of the four suggested above. All incorrect sentences contain only one type of error. Consider a sentence correct if it contains none of the types of errors mentioned, although there may be other correct ways of expressing the same thought.

1. Mrs. Black the supervisor of the unit, has many important duties.   1._____

2. We spoke to the man whom you saw yesterday.   2._____

3. When a holiday falls on Sunday, it is officially celebrated on monday.   3._____

4. Of the two reports submitted, this one is the best.   4._____

5. Each staff member, including the accountants, were invited to the meeting.   5._____

6. Give the package to whomever calls for it.   6._____

7. To plan the work is our responsibility; to carry it out is his.   7._____

8. "May I see the person in charge of this office," asked the visitor?   8._____

9. He knows that it was not us who prepared the report.   9._____

10. These problems were brought to the attention of senator Johnson.   10._____

11. The librarian classifies all books periodicals and documents.   11._____

12. Any employee who uses an adding machine realizes its importance.   12._____

13. Instead of coming to the office, the clerk should of come to the supply room.   13._____

14. He asked, "will your staff assist us?"   14._____

15. Having been posted on the bulletin board, we were certain that the announcements would be read.   15._____

16. He was not informed, that he would have to work overtime.   16._____

17. The wind blew several papers off of his desk.   17._____

18. Charles Dole, who is a member of the committee, was asked to confer with commissioner Wilson.   18._____

19. Miss Bell will issue a copy to whomever asks for one.   19._____

20. Most employees, and he is no exception do not like to work overtime.   20.____

21. This is the man whom you interviewed last week.   21.____

22. Of the two cities visited, White Plains is the cleanest.   22.____

23. Although he was willing to work on other holidays, he refused to work on Labor day.   23.____

24. If an employee wishes to attend the conference, he should fill out the necessary forms.   24.____

25. The division chief reports that an engineer and an inspector is needed for this special survey.   25.____

———

KEY (CORRECT ANSWERS)

1.	B	11.	B
2.	D	12.	D
3.	C	13.	A
4.	A	14.	C
5.	A	15.	A
6.	A	16.	B
7.	D	17.	A
8.	B	18.	C
9.	A	19.	A
10.	C	20.	B

21.	D
22.	A
23.	C
24.	D
25.	A

———

TEST 3

1.   We have learned that there was more than twelve people present at the meeting.　　1._____

2.   Every one of the employees is able to do this kind of work.　　2._____

3.   Neither the supervisor nor his assistant are in the office today.　　3._____

4.   The office manager announced that any clerk, who volunteered for the assignment, would be rewarded.　　4._____

5.   After looking carefully in all the files, the letter was finally found on a desk.　　5._____

6.   In answer to the clerk's question, the supervisor said, "this assignment must be completed today."　　6._____

7.   The office manager says that he can permit only you and me to go to the meeting.　　7._____

8.   The supervisor refused to state who he would assign to the reception unit.　　8._____

9.   At the last meeting, he said that he would interview us in September.　　9._____

10.   Mr. Jones, who is one of our most experienced employees has been placed in charge of the main office.　　10._____

11.   I think that this adding machine is the most useful of the two we have in our office.　　11._____

12.   Between you and I, our new stenographer is not as competent as our former stenographer.　　12._____

13.   The new assignment should be given to whoever can do the work rapidly.　　13._____

14.   Mrs. Smith, as well as three other typists, was assigned to the new office.　　14._____

15.   The staff assembled for the conference on time but, the main speaker arrived late.　　15._____

16.   The work was assigned to Miss Green and me.　　16._____

17.   The staff regulations state that an employee, who is frequently tardy, may receive a negative evaluation.　　17._____

18.   He is the kind of person who is always willing to undertake difficult assignments.　　18._____

19. Mr. Wright's request cannot be granted under no conditions.   19.____

20. George Colt a new employee, was asked to deliver the report to the Domestic Relations   20.____
Court.

21. The supervisor entered the room and said, "The work must be completed today."   21.____

22. The employees were given their assignments and, they were asked to begin work imme-   22.____
diately.

23. The letter will be sent to the United States senate this week.   23.____

24. When the supervisor entered the room, he noticed that the book was laying on the desk.   24.____

25. The price of the pens were higher than the price of the pencils.   25.____

KEY (CORRECT ANSWERS)

1.	A		11.	A
2.	D		12.	A
3.	A		13.	D
4.	B		14.	D
5.	A		15.	B
6.	C		16.	D
7.	D		17.	B
8.	A		18.	D
9.	C		19.	A
10.	B		20.	B

21.	D
22.	B
23.	C
24.	A
25.	A

PREPARING WRITTEN MATERIAL

PARAGRAPH REARRANGEMENT
COMMENTARY

The sentences which follow are in scrambled order. You are to rearrange them in proper order and indicate the letter choice containing the correct answer at the space at the right.

Each group of sentences in this section is actually a paragraph presented in scrambled order. Each sentence in the group has a place in that paragraph; no sentence is to be left out. You are to read each group of sentences and decide upon the best order in which to put the sentences so as to form as well-organized paragraph.

The questions in this section measure the ability to solve a problem when all the facts relevant to its solution are not given.

More specifically, certain positions of responsibility and authority require the employee to discover connections between events sometimes, apparently, unrelated. In order to do this, the employee will find it necessary to correctly infer that unspecified events have probably occurred or are likely to occur. This ability becomes especially important when action must be taken on incomplete information.

Accordingly, these questions require competitors to choose among several suggested alternatives, each of which presents a different sequential arrangement of the events. Competitors must choose the MOST logical of the suggested sequences.

In order to do so, they may be required to draw on general knowledge to infer missing concepts or events that are essential to sequencing the given events. Competitors should be careful to infer only what is essential to the sequence. The plausibility of the wrong alternatives will always require the inclusion of unlikely events or of additional chains of events which are NOT essential to sequencing the given events.

It's very important to remember that you are looking for the best of the four possible choices, and that the best choice of all may not even be one of the answers you're given to choose from.

There is no one right way to these problems. Many people have found it helpful to first write out the order of the sentences, as they would have arranged them, on their scrap paper before looking at the possible answers. If their optimum answer is there, this can save them some time. If it isn't, this method can still give insight into solving the problem. Others find it most helpful to just go through each of the possible choices, contrasting each as they go along. You should use whatever method feels comfortable, and works, for you.

While most of these types of questions are not that difficult, we've added a higher percentage of the difficult type, just to give you more practice. Usually there are only one or two questions on this section that contain such subtle distinctions that you're unable to answer confidently, and you then may find yourself stuck deciding between two possible choices, neither of which you're sure about.

EXAMINATION SECTION
TEST 1

DIRECTIONS: The sentences that follow are in scrambled order. You are to rearrange them in proper order and indicate the letter choice containing the correct answer. *PRINT THE LETTER OF THE CORRECT ANSWER IN THE SPACE AT THE RIGHT.*

1. Below are four statements labeled W., X., Y., and Z.   1.____
   W.   He was a strict and fanatic drillmaster.
   X.   The word is always used in a derogatory sense and generally shows resentment and anger on the part of the user.
   Y.   It is from the name of this Frenchman that we derive our English word, martinet.
   Z.   Jean Martinet was the Inspector-General of Infantry during the reign of King Louis XIV.

   The *PROPER* order in which these sentences should be placed in a paragraph is:

   A.   X, Z, W, Y   B.   X, Z, Y, W   C.   Z, W, Y, X   D.   Z, Y, W, X

2. In the following paragraph, the sentences which are numbered, have been jumbled.   2.____
   1.   Since then it has undergone changes.
   2.   It was incorporated in 1955 under the laws of the State of New York.
   3.   Its primary purpose, a cleaner city, has, however, remained the same.
   4.   The Citizens Committee works in cooperation with the Mayor's Inter-departmental Committee for a Clean City.

   The order in which these sentences should be arranged to form a well-organized paragraph is:

   A.   2, 4, 1, 3   B.   3, 4, 1, 2   C.   4, 2, 1, 3   D.   4, 3, 2, 1

Questions 3-5.

DIRECTIONS: The sentences listed below are part of a meaningful paragraph but they are not given in their proper order. You are to decide what would be the *best order* in which to put the sentences so as to form a well-organized paragraph. Each sentence has a place in the paragraph; there are no extra sentences. You are then to answer questions 3 to 5 inclusive on the basis of your rearrangements of these secrambled sentences into a properly organized paragraph.

In 1887 some insurance companies organized an Inspection Department to advise their clients on all phases of fire prevention and protection. Probably this has been due to the smaller annual fire losses in Great Britain than in the United States. It tests various fire prevention devices and appliances and determines manufacturing hazards and their safeguards. Fire research began earlier in the United States and is more advanced than in Great Britain. Later they established a laboratory specializing in electrical, mechanical, hydraulic, and chemical fields.

3. When the five sentences are arranged in proper order, the paragraph starts with the sen-   3._____
   tence which begins

   A. "In 1887 ..."   B. "Probably this ..."   C. "It tests ..."
   D. "Fire research ..."   E. "Later they ..."

4. In the last sentence listed above, "they" refers to   4._____

   A. insurance companies
   B. the United States and Great Britain
   C. the Inspection Department
   D. clients
   E. technicians

5. When the above paragraph is properly arranged, it ends with the words   5._____

   A. "... and protection."   B. "... the United States."
   C. "... their safeguards."   D. "... in Great Britain."
   E. "... chemical fields."

___

KEY (CORRECT ANSWERS)

1. C
2. C
3. D
4. A
5. C

___

TEST 2

DIRECTIONS: In each of the questions numbered 1 through 5, several sentences are given. For each question, choose as your answer the group of numbers that represents the *most logical* order of these sentences if they were arranged in paragraph form. *PRINT THE LETTER OF THE CORRECT ANSWER IN THE SPACE AT THE RIGHT.*

1. 1. It is established when one shows that the landlord has prevented the tenant's enjoyment of his interest in the property leased.
   2. Constructive eviction is the result of a breach of the covenant of quiet enjoyment implied in all leases.
   3. In some parts of the United States, it is not complete until the tenant vacates within a reasonable time.
   4. Generally, the acts must be of such serious and permanent character as to deny the tenant the enjoyment of his possessing rights.
   5. In this event, upon abandonment of the premises, the tenant's liability for that ceases.

   The CORRECT answer is:

   A. 2, 1, 4, 3, 5 B. 5, 2, 3, 1, 4 C. 4, 3, 1, 2, 5
   D. 1, 3, 5, 4, 2

   1.____

2. 1. The powerlessness before private and public authorities that is the typical experience of the slum tenant is reminiscent of the situation of blue-collar workers all through the nineteenth century.
   2. Similarly, in recent years, this chapter of history has been reopened by anti-poverty groups which have attempted to organize slum tenants to enable them to bargain collectively with their landlords about the conditions of their tenancies.
   3. It is familiar history that many of the workers remedied their condition by joining together and presenting their demands collectively.
   4. Like the workers, tenants are forced by the conditions of modern life into substantial dependence on these who possess great political arid economic power.
   5. What's more, the very fact of dependence coupled with an absence of education and self-confidence makes them hesitant and unable to stand up for what they need from those in power.

   The CORRECT answer is:

   A. 5, 4, 1, 2, 3 B. 2, 3, 1, 5, 4 C. 3, 1, 5, 4, 2
   D. 1, 4, 5, 3, 2

   2.____

3. 1. A railroad, for example, when not acting as a common carrier may contract; away responsibility for its own negligence.
   2. As to a landlord, however, no decision has been found relating to the legal effect of a clause shifting the statutory duty of repair to the tenant.
   3. The courts have not passed on the validity of clauses relieving the landlord of this duty and liability.
   4. They have, however, upheld the validity of exculpatory clauses in other types of contracts.
   5. Housing regulations impose a duty upon the landlord to maintain leased premises in safe condition.

   3.____

6. As another example, a bailee may limit his liability except for gross negligence, willful acts, or fraud.

The CORRECT answer is:

A. 2, 1, 6, 4, 3, 5   B. 1, 3, 4, 5, 6, 2   C. 3, 5, 1, 4, 2, 6
D. 5, 3, 4, 1, 6, 2

4.   1. Since there are only samples in the building, retail or consumer sales are generally eschewed by mart occupants, and,in some instances, rigid controls are maintained to limit entrance to the mart only to those persons engaged in retailing.   4.____

     2. Since World War I, in many larger cities, there has developed a new type of property, called the mart building.

     3. It can, therefore, be used by wholesalers and jobbers for the display of sample merchandise.

     4. This type of building is most frequently a multi-storied, finished interior property which is a cross between a retail arcade and a loft building.

     5. This limitation enables the mart occupants to ship the orders from another location after the retailer or dealer makes his selection from the samples.

The CORRECT answer is:

A. 2, 4, 3, 1, 5   B. 4, 3, 5, 1, 2   C. 1, 3, 2, 4, 5
D. 1, 4, 2, 3, 5

5.   1. In general, staff-line friction reduces the distinctive contribution of staff personnel.   5.____

     2. The conflicts, however, introduce an uncontrolled element into the managerial system.

     3. On the other hand, the natural resistance of the line to staff innovations probably usefully restrains over-eager efforts to apply untested procedures on a large scale.

     4. Under such conditions, it is difficult to know when valuable ideas are being sacrificed.

     5. The relatively weak position of staff, requiring accommodation to the line, tends to restrict their ability to engage .in free, experimental innovation.

The CORRECT answer is:

A. 4, 2, 3, 1, 3   B. 1, 5, 3, 2, 4   C. 5, 3, 1, 2, 4
D. 2, 1, 4, 5, 3

KEY (CORRECT ANSWERS)

1. A
2. D
3. D
4. A
5. B

TEST 3

DIRECTIONS: Questions 1 through 4 consist of six sentences which can be arranged in a logical sequence. For each question, select the choice which places the numbered sentences in the *most logical* sequence. *PRINT THE LETTER OF THE CORRECT ANSWER IN THE SPACE AT THE RIGHT.*

1.   1. The burden of proof as to each issue is determined before trial and remains upon the same party throughout the trial.   1.____

    2. The jury is at liberty to believe one witness' testimony as against a number of contradictory witnesses.

    3. In a civil case, the party bearing the burden of proof is required to prove his contention by a fair preponderance of the evidence.

    4. However, it must be noted that a fair preponderance of evidence does not necessarily mean a greater number of witnesses.

    5. The burden of proof is the burden which rests upon one of the parties to an action to persuade the trier of the facts, generally the jury, that a proposition he asserts is true.

    6. If the evidence is equally balanced, or if it leaves the jury in such doubt as to be unable to decide the controversy either way, judgment must be given against the party upon whom the burden of proof rests.

The CORRECT answer is:

A. 3, 2, 5, 4, 1, 6   B. 1, 2, 6, 5, 3, 4   C. 3, 4, 5, 1, 2, 6
D. 5, 1, 3, 6, 4, 2

2.   1. If a parent is without assets and is unemployed, he cannot be convicted of the crime of non-support of a child.   2.____

    2. The term "sufficient ability" has been held to mean sufficient financial ability.

    3. It does not matter if his unemployment is by choice or unavoidable circumstances.

    4. If he fails to take any steps at all, he may be liable to prosecution for endangering the welfare of a child.

    5. Under the penal law, a parent is responsible for the support of his minor child only if the parent is "of sufficient ability."

    6. An indigent parent may meet his obligation by borrowing money or by seeking aid under the provisions of the Social Welfare Law.

The CORRECT answer is:

A. 6, 1, 5, 3, 2, 4   B. 1, 3, 5, 2, 4, 6   C. 5, 2, 1, 3, 6, 4
D. 1, 6, 4, 5, 2, 3

3.   1.   Consider, for example, the case of a rabble rouser who urges a group of twenty   3.____
          people to go out and break the windows of a nearby factory.
      2.   Therefore, the law fills the indicated gap with the crime of inciting to riot."
      3.   A person is considered guilty of inciting to riot when he urges ten or more per-
          sons to engage in tumultuous and violent conduct of a kind likely to create public
          alarm.
      4.   However, if he has not obtained the cooperation of at least four people, he can-
          not be charged with unlawful assembly.
      5.   The charge of inciting to riot was added to the law to cover types of conduct
          which cannot be classified as either the crime of "riot" or the crime of "unlawful
          assembly."
      6.   If he acquires the acquiescence of at least four of them, he is guilty of unlawful
          assembly even if the project does not materialize.
      The CORRECT answer is:

      A.   3, 5, 1, 6, 4, 2   B.   5, 1, 4, 6, 2, 3   C.   3, 4, 1, 5, 2, 6
      D.   5, 1, 4, 6, 3, 2

4.   1.   If, however, the rebuttal evidence presents an issue of credibility, it is for the jury to   4.____
          determine whether the presumption has, in fact, been destroyed.
      2.   Once sufficient evidence to the contrary is introduced, the presumption disap-
          pears from the trial.
      3.   The effect of a presumption is to place the burden upon the adversary to come
          forward with evidence to rebut the presumption.
      4.   When a presumption is overcome and ceases to exist in the case, the fact or
          facts which gave rise to the presumption still remain.
      5.   Whether a presumption has been overcome is ordinarily a question for the court.
      6.   Such information may furnish a basis for a logical inference.
      The CORRECT answer is:

      A.   4, 6, 2, 5, 1, 3   B.   3, 2, 5, 1, 4, 6   C.   5, 3, 6, 4, 2, 1
      D.   5, 4, 1, 2, 6, 3

_____

KEY (CORRECT ANSWERS)

1.   D
2.   C
3.   A
4.   B

REPORT WRITING
EXAMINATION SECTION
TEST 1

DIRECTIONS: Each question or incomplete statement is followed by several suggested answers or completions. Select the one that BEST answers the question or completes the statement. *PRINT THE LETTER OF THE CORRECT ANSWER IN THE SPACE AT THE RIGHT.*

Questions 1-4.

DIRECTIONS: Answer Questions 1 through 4 on the basis of the following report which was prepared by a supervisor for inclusion in his agency's annual report.

Line
#

1   On Oct. 13, I was assigned to study the salaries paid
2   to clerical employees in various titles by the city and by
3   private industry in the area.
4   In order to get the data I needed, I called Mr. Johnson at
5   the Bureau of the Budget and the payroll officers at X Corp.—
6   a brokerage house, Y Co.—an insurance company, and Z Inc.—
7   a publishing firm. None of them was available and I had to call
8   all of them again the next day.
9   When I finally got the information I needed, I drew up a
10   chart, which is attached. Note that not all of the companies I
11   contacted employed people at all the different levels used in the
12   city service.
13   The conclusions I draw from analyzing this information is
14   as follows: The city's entry-level salary is about average for
15   the region; middle-level salaries are generally higher in the
16   city government than in private industry; but salaries at the
17   highest levels in private industry are better than city em-
18   ployees' pay.

1. Which of the following criticisms about the style in which this report is written is *most valid*?   1.____

    A. It is too informal.   B. It is too concise.
    C. It is too choppy.   D. The syntax is too complex.

2. Judging from the statements made in the report, the method followed by this employee in performing his research was   2.____

    A. *good;* he contacted a representative sample of businesses in the area
    B. *poor;* he should have drawn more definite conclusions
    C. *good;* he was persistent in collecting information
    D. *poor;* he did not make a thorough study

3. One sentence in this report contains a grammatical error. This sentence *begins* on line   3.____
number

    A. 4   B. 7   C. 10   D. 13

4. The type of information given in this report which should be presented in footnotes or in   4.____
an appendix, is the

    A. purpose of the study
    B. specifics about the businesses contacted
    C. reference to the chart
    D. conclusions drawn by the author

5. The use of a graph to show statistical data in a report is *superior* to a table because it   5.____

    A. features approximations
    B. emphasizes facts and relationships more dramatically
    C. C. presents data more accurately
    D. is easily understood by the average reader

6. Of the following, the degree of formality required of a written report in tone is *most likely*   6.____
to depend on the

    A. subject matter of the report
    B. frequency of its occurrence
    C. amount of time available for its preparation
    D. audience for whom the report is intended

7. Of the following, a distinguishing characteristic of a written report intended for the head   7.____
of your agency as compared to a report prepared for a lower-echelon staff member, is
that the report for the agency head should *usually* include

    A. considerably more detail, especially statistical data
    B. the essential details in an abbreviated form
    C. all available source material
    D. an annotated bibliography

8. Assume that you are asked to write a lengthy report for use by the administrator of your   8.____
agency, the subject of which is "The Impact of Proposed New Data Processing Operations on Line Personnel" in your agency. You decide that the *most appropriate* type of
report for you to prepare is an analytical report, including recommendations.
The MAIN reason for your decision is that

    A. the subject of the report is extremely complex
    B. large sums of money are involved
    C. the report is being prepared for the administrator
    D. you intend to include charts and graphs

9. Assume that you are preparing a report based on a survey dealing with the attitudes of employees in Division X regarding proposed new changes in compensating employees for working overtime. Three per cent of the respondents to the survey voluntarily offer an unfavorable opinion on the method of assigning overtime work, a question not specifically asked of the employees.
On the basis of this information, the *most appropriate* and *significant* of the following comments for you to make in the report with regard to employees' attitudes on assigning overtime work, is that

    9.____

    A. an insignificant percentage of employees dislike the method of assigning overtime work
    B. three per cent of the employees in Division X dislike the method of assigning overtime work
    C. three per cent of the sample selected for the survey voiced an unfavorable opinion on the method of assigning overtime work
    D. some employees voluntarily voiced negative feelings about the method of assigning overtime work, making it impossible to determine the extent of this attitude

10. A supervisor should be able to prepare a report that is well-written and unambiguous. Of the following sentences that might appear in a report, select the one which communicates *most clearly* the intent of its author.

    10.____

    A. When your subordinates speak to a group of people, they should be well-informed.
    B. When he asked him to leave, SanMan King told him that he would refuse the request.
    C. Because he is a good worker, Foreman Jefferson assigned Assistant Foreman D'Agostino to replace him.
    D. Each of us is responsible for the actions of our subordinates.

11. In some reports, especially longer ones, a list of the resources (books, papers, magazines, etc.) used to prepare it is included. This list is called the

    11.____

    A. accreditation   B. bibliography
    C. summary   D. glossary

12. Reports are usually divided into several sections, some of which are more necessary than others.
Of the following, the section which is ABSOLUTELY necessary to include in a report is

    12.____

    A. a table of contents   B. the body
    C. an index   D. a bibliography

13. Suppose you are writing a report on an interview you have just completed with a particularly hostile applicant. Which of the following BEST describes what you should include in this report?

    13.____

    A. What you think caused the applicant's hostile attitude during the interview
    B. Specific examples of the applicant's hostile remarks and behavior
    C. The relevant information uncovered during the interview
    D. A recommendation that the applicant's request be denied because of his hostility

14. When including recommendations in a report to your supervisor, which of the following is MOST important for you to do?   14.___

    A. Provide several alternative courses of action for each recommendation
    B. First present the supporting evidence, then the recommendations
    C. First present the recommendations, then the supporting evidence
    D. Make sure the recommendations arise logically out of the information in the report

15. It is often necessary that the writer of a report present facts and sufficient arguments to gain acceptance of the points, conclusions, or recommendations set forth in the report. Of the following, the LEAST advisable step to take in organizing a report, when such argumentation is the important factor, is a(n)   15.___

    A. elaborate expression of personal belief
    B. businesslike discussion of the problem as a whole
    C. orderly arrangement of convincing data
    D. reasonable explanation of the primary issues

16. In some types of reports, visual aids add interest, meaning, and support. They also pro- vide an essential means of effectively communicating the message of the report. Of the following, the selection of the suitable visual aids to use with a report is LEAST dependent on the   16.___

    A. nature and scope of the report
    B. way in which the aid is to be used
    C. aids used in other reports
    D. prospective readers of the report

17. Visual aids used in a report may be placed either in the text material or in the appendix. Deciding where to put a chart, table, or any such aid *should* depend on the   17.___

    A. title of the report   B. purpose of the visual aid
    C. title of the visual aid   D. length of the report

18. A report is often revised several times before final preparation and distribution in an effort to make certain the report meets the needs of the situation for which it is designed. Which of the following is the BEST way for the author to be sure that a report covers the areas he intended?   18.___

    A. Obtain a co-worker's opinion
    B. Compare it with a content checklist
    C. Test it on a subordinate
    D. Check his bibliography

19. In which of the following situations is an oral report preferable to a written report? When a(n)   19.___

    A. recommendation is being made for a future plan of action
    B. department head requests immediate information
    C. long standing policy change is made
    D. analysis of complicated statistical data is involved

20. When an applicant is approved, the supervisor must fill in standard forms with certain   20.____
information.
The GREATEST advantage of using standard forms in this situation rather than having
the supervisor write the report as he sees fit, is that

    A. the report can be acted on quickly
    B. the report can be written without directions from a supervisor
    C. needed information is less likely to be left out of the report
    D. information that is written up this way is more likely to be verified

21. Assume that it is part of your job to prepare a monthly report for your unit head that even-   21.____
tually goes to the director. The report contains information on the number of applicants
you have interviewed that have been approved and the number of applicants you have
interviewed that have been turned down.
Errors on such reports are serious because

    A. you are expected to be able to prove how many applicants you have interviewed
       each month
    B. accurate statistics are needed for effective management of the department
    C. they may not be discovered before the report is transmitted to the director
    D. they may result in loss to the applicants left out of the report

22. The frequency with which job reports are submitted should depend MAINLY on   22.____

    A. how comprehensive the report has to be
    B. the amount of information in the report
    C. the availability of an experienced man to write the report
    D. the importance of changes in the information included in the report

23. The CHIEF purpose in preparing an outline for a report is *usually* to insure that   23.____

    A. the report will be grammatically correct
    B. every point will be given equal emphasis
    C. principal and secondary points will be properly integrated
    D. the language of the report will be of the same level and include the same technical
       terms

24. The MAIN reason for requiring written job reports is to   24.____

    A. avoid the necessity of oral orders
    B. develop better methods of doing the work
    C. provide a permanent record of what was done
    D. increase the amount of work that can be done

25. Assume you are recommending in a report to your supervisor that a radical change in a   25.____
standard maintenance procedure should be adopted.
Of the following, the MOST important information to be included in this report is

    A. a list of the reasons for making this change
    B. the names of others who favor the change
    C. a complete description of the present procedure
    D. amount of training time needed for the new procedure

KEY (CORRECT ANSWERS)

1.	A	11.	B
2.	D	12.	B
3.	D	13.	C
4.	B	14.	D
5.	B	15.	A
6.	D	16.	C
7.	B	17.	B
8.	A	18.	B
9.	D	19.	B
10.	D	20.	C

21.	B
22.	D
23.	C
24.	C
25.	A

———

TEST 2

1. It is often necessary that the writer of a report present facts and sufficient arguments to gain acceptance of the points, conclusions, or recommendations set forth in the report. Of the following, the LEAST advisable step to take in organizing a report, when such argumentation is the important factor, is a(n)   1.____

   A. elaborate expression of personal belief
   B. businesslike discussion of the problem as a whole
   C. orderly arrangement of convincing data
   D. reasonable explanation of the primary issues

2. Of the following, the factor which is generally considered to be LEAST characteristic of a good control report is that it   2.____

   A. stresses performance that adheres to standard rather than emphasizing the exception
   B. supplies information intended to serve as the basis for corrective action
   C. provides feedback for the planning process
   D. includes data that reflect trends as well as current status

3. An administrative assistant has been asked by his superior to write a concise, factual report with objective conclusions and recommendations based on facts assembled by other researchers.
   Of the following factors, the administrative assistant should give LEAST consideratio to   3.____

   A. the educational level of the person or persons for whom the report is being prepared
   B. the use to be made of the report
   C. the complexity of the problem
   D. his own feelings about the importance of the problem

4. When making a written report, it is often recommended that the findings or conclusions be presented near the beginning of the report.
   Of the following, the MOST important reason for doing this is that it   4.____

   A. facilitates organizing the material clearly
   B. assures that all the topics will be covered
   C. avoids unnecessary repetition of ideas
   D. prepares the reader for the facts that will follow

5. You have been asked to write a report on methods of hiring and training new employees. Your report is going to be about ten pages long.
   For the convenience of your readers, a brief summary of your findings *should*   5.____

   A. appear at the beginning of your report
   B. be appended to the report as a postscript
   C. be circulated in a separate memo
   D. be inserted in tabular form in the middle of your report

6. In preparing a report, the MAIN reason for writing an outline is *usually* to   6.____

    A. help organize thoughts in a logical sequence
    B. provide a guide for the typing of the report
    C. allow the ultimate user to review the report in advance
    D. ensure that the report is being prepared on schedule

7. The one of the following which is *most appropriate* as a reason for including footnotes in a report is to   7.____

    A. correct capitalization   B. delete passages
    C. improve punctuation   D. cite references

8. A completed formal report may contain all of the following EXCEPT   8.____

    A. a synopsis   B. a preface
    C. marginal notes   D. bibliographical references

9. Of the following, the MAIN use of proofreaders' marks is to   9.____

    A. explain corrections to be made
    B. indicate that a manuscript has been read and approved
    C. let the reader know who proofread the report
    D. indicate the format of the report

10. Informative, readable and concise reports have been found to observe the following rules: 10.____
    Rule I.   Keep the report short and easy to understand.
    Rule II.   Vary the length of sentences.
    Rule III.   Vary the style of sentences so that, for example, they are not all just subject-verb, subject-verb.
Consider this hospital laboratory report: The experiment was started in January. The apparatus was put together in six weeks. At that time the synthesizing process was begun. The synthetic chemicals were separated. Then they were used in tests on patients.
Which one of the following choices MOST accurately classifies the above rules into those which are *violated* by this report and those which are *not*?

    A. II is violated, but I and III are not.
    B. III is violated, but I and II are not.
    C. II and III are violated, but I is not.
    D. I, II, and III are violated.

Questions 11-13.

DIRECTIONS: Questions 11 through 13 are based on the following example of a report. The report consists of eight numbered sentences, some of which are not consistent with the principles of good report writing.

(1) I interviewed Mrs. Loretta Crawford in Room 424 of County Hospital. (2) She had collapsed on the street and been brought into emergency. (3) She is an attractive woman with many friends judging by the cards she had received. (4) She did not know what her husband's last job had been, or what their present income was. (5) The first thing that Mrs. Crawford said was that she had never worked and that her husband was presently unemployed. (6) She did not know if they had any medical coverage or if they could pay the bill. (7) She said that her husband could not be reached by telephone but that he would be in to see her that afternoon. (8) I left word at the nursing station to be called when he arrived.

11. A good report should be arranged in logical order. Which of the following sentences from the report does NOT appear in its proper sequence in the report? Sentence

11.____

    A. 1   B. 4   C. 7   D. 8

12. Only material that is relevant to the main thought of a report should be included. Which of the following sentences from the report contains material which is LEAST relevant to this report? Sentence

12.____

    A. 3   B. 4   C. 6   D. 8

13. Reports should include all essential information.
Of the following, the MOST important fact that is *missing* from this report is:

13.____

    A. Who was involved in the interview
    B. What was discovered at the interview
    C. When the interview took place
    D. Where the interview took place

Questions 14-15.

DIRECTIONS: Each of Questions 14 and 15 consists of four numbered sentences which constitute a paragraph in a report. They are not in the right order. Choose the numbered arrangement appearing after letter A, B, C, or D which is MOST logical and which BEST expresses the thought of the paragraph.

14.   I.   Congress made the commitment explicit in the Housing Act of 1949, establishing as a national goal the realization of a decent home and suitable environment for every American family.

14.____

    II.   The result has been that the goal of decent home and suitable environment is still as far distant as ever for the disadvantaged urban family.
    III.   In spite of this action by Congress, federal housing programs have continued to be fragmented and grossly under-funded.
    IV.   The passage of the National Housing Act signaled a new federal commitment to provide housing for the nation's citizens.

    A. I, IV, III, II   B. IV, I, III, II
    C. IV, I, II, III   D. II, IV, I, III

15. I.   The greater expense does not necessarily involve "exploitation," but it is often per-
          ceived as exploitative and unfair by those who are aware of the price differences
          involved, but unaware of operating costs.
     II. Ghetto residents believe they are "exploited" by local merchants, and evidence
          substantiates some of these beliefs.
     III. However, stores in low-income areas were more likely to be small independents,
          which could not achieve the economies available to supermarket chains and
          were, therefore, more likely to charge higher prices, and the customers were
          more likely to buy smaller-sized packages which are more expensive per unit of
          measure.
     IV. A study conducted in one city showed that distinctly higher prices were charged
          for goods sold in ghetto stores than in other areas.

     A.   IV, II, I, III   B.   IV, I, III, II
     C.   II, IV, III, I   D.   II, III, IV, I

15.____

16. In organizing data to be presented in a formal report, the FIRST of the following steps
     should be

     A.   determining the conclusions to be drawn
     B.   establishing the time sequence of the data
     C.   sorting and arranging like data into groups
     D.   evaluating how consistently the data support the recommendations

16.____

17. All reports should be prepared with *at least* one copy so that

     A.   there is one copy for your file
     B.   there is a copy for your supervisor
     C.   the report can be sent to more than one person
     D.   the person getting the report can forward a copy to someone else

17.____

18. Before turning in a report of an investigation he has made, a supervisor discovers some
     additional information he did not include in this report.
     Whether he rewrites this report to include this additional information should PRIMA-
     RILY depend on the

     A.   importance of the report itself
     B.   number of people who will eventually review this report
     C.   established policy covering the subject matter of the report
     D.   bearing this new information has on the conclusions of the report

18.____

———————

KEY (CORRECT ANSWERS)

1.	A		11.	B
2.	A		12.	A
3.	D		13.	C
4.	D		14.	B
5.	A		15.	C
6.	A		16.	C
7.	D		17.	A
8.	C		18.	D
9.	A			
10.	C			

INTERVIEWING
EXAMINATION SECTION
TEST 1

DIRECTIONS: Each question or incomplete statement is followed by several suggested answers or completions. Select the one that BEST answers the question or completes the statement. *PRINT THE LETTER OF THE CORRECT ANSWER IN THE SPACE AT THE RIGHT.*

1. Of the methods given below for obtaining desired information from applicants, the one considered the BEST interviewing method is to 1.____

   A. work from an outline, asking the questions in the order in which they appear and requiring the applicant to give specific answers
   B. let the applicant tell what he has to say in his own way first, the interviewer then taking responsibility for asking questions on points not covered
   C. tell the applicant all the facts that it is necessary to have, then letting him give the information in any way he chooses
   D. verify all such facts as birth date, income, and past employment before seeing the applicant, then asking the applicant to fill in the remaining gaps when he is interviewed

2. Suppose an applicant objects to answering a question regarding his recent employment and asks, "What business is it of yours, young man?" 2.____
In conducting the interview, the MOST constructive course of action for you to take under the circumstances would be to

   A. tell the applicant you have no intention of prying into his personal affairs and go on to the next question
   B. refer the applicant to your supervisor
   C. rephrase the question so that only a "Yes" or "No" answer is required
   D. explain why the question is being asked

3. An interview is BEST conducted in private PRIMARILY because 3.____

   A. the person interviewed will tend to be less self-conscious
   B. the interviewer will be able to maintain his continuity of thought better
   C. it will insure that the interview is "off the record"
   D. people tend to "show off" before an audience

4. An interviewer will be better able to understand the person interviewed and his problems if he recognizes that much of the person's behavior is due to *motives* 4.____

   A. which are deliberate   B. of which he is unaware
   C. which are inexplicable   D. which are kept under contrc

5. When an applicant is repeatedly told that "everything will be all right," the effect that can *usually* be expected is that he will 5.____

   A. develop overt negativistic reactions toward the agency
   B. become too closely identified with the interviewer
   C. doubt the interviewer's ability to understand and help with his problems
   D. have greater confidence in the interviewer

6. While interviewing a client, it is *preferable* that the interviewer   6.____

    A. take no notes in order to avoid disturbing the client
    B. focus primary attention on the client while the client is talking
    C. take no notes in order to impress upon the client the interviewer's ability to remember all the pertinent facts of his case
    D. record all the details in order to show the client that what he says is important

7. During an interview, a curious applicant asks several questions about the interviewer's   7.____
private life. As the interviewer, you should

    A. refuse to answer such questions
    B. answer his questions fully
    C. explain that your primary concern is with his problems and that discussion of your personal affairs will not be helpful in meeting his needs
    D. explain that it is the responsibility of the interviewer to ask questions and not to answer them

8. An interviewer can BEST establish a good relationship with the person being interviewed   8.____
by

    A. assuming casual interest in the statements made by the person being interviewed
    B. asking questions which enable the person to show pride in his knowledge
    C. taking the point of view of the person interviewed
    D. showing a genuine interest in the person

9. An interviewer's attention must be directed toward himself as well as toward the person   9.____
interviewed.
This statement *means* that the interviewer should

    A. keep in mind the extent to which his own prejudices may influence his judgment
    B. rationalize the statements made by the person interviewed
    C. gain the respect and confidence of the person interviewed
    D. avoid being too impersonal

10. *More* complete expression will be obtained from a person being interviewed if the inter-   10.____
viewer can create the impression that

    A. the data secured will become part of a permanent record
    B. official information must be accurate in every detail
    C. it is the duty of the person interviewed to give accurate data
    D. the person interviewed is participating in a discussion of his own problems

11. The practice of asking leading questions should be *avoided* in an interview because the   11.____

    A. interviewer risks revealing his attitudes to the person being interviewed
    B. interviewer may be led to ignore the objective attitudes of the person interviewed
    C. answers may be unwarrantedly influenced
    D. person interviewed will resent the attempt to lead him and will be less cooperative

12. A *good* technique for the interviewer to use in an effort to secure reliable data and to reduce the possibility of misunderstanding is to   12._____

    A. use casual undirected conversation, enabling the person being interviewed to talk about himself, and thus secure the desired information
    B. adopt the procedure of using direct questions regularly
    C. extract the desired information from the person being interviewed by putting him on the defensive
    D. explain to the person being interviewed the information desired and the reason for needing it

13. In interviewing an applicant, your attitude toward his veracity *should be* that the information he has furnished you is   13._____

    A. *untruthful* until you have had an opportunity to check the information
    B. *truthful* only insofar as verifiable facts are concerned
    C. *untruthful* because clients tend to interpret everything in their own favor
    D. *truthful* until you have information to the contrary

14. When an agency assigns its most experienced interviewers to conduct initial interviews with applicants, the MOST important reason for its action is that   14._____

    A. experienced workers are always older, and therefore, command the respect of applicants
    B. the applicant may be given a complete understanding of the procedures to be followed and the time involved in obtaining assistance
    C. applicants with fraudulent intentions will be detected, and prevented from obtaining further services from the agency
    D. the applicant may be given an understanding of the purpose of the assistance program and of the bases for granting assistance, in addition to the routine information

15. In conducting the *first* interview with an applicant, you should   15._____

    A. ask questions requiring "yes" or "no" answers in order to simplify the interview
    B. rephrase several of the key questions as a check on his previous statements
    C. let him tell his own story while keeping him to the relevant facts
    D. avoid showing any sympathy for the applicant while he is revealing his personal needs and problems

16. When an interviewer opens an interview by asking the client direct questions about his work, it is *very* likely that the client will feel   16._____

    A. that the interviewer is interested in him
    B. at ease if his work has been good
    C. free to discuss his attitudes toward his work
    D. that good reports are of great importance to the interviewer in his thinking

17. When an interviewer does NOT understand the meaning of a response that a client has made, the interviewer should   17._____

    A. proceed to another topic
    B. state that he does not understand and ask for clarification
    C. act as if he understands so that the client's confidence in him should not be shaken
    D. ask the client to rephrase his response

18. When an interviewer makes a response which brings on a high degree of resistance in the client, he should

    A. apologize and rephrase his remark in a less evocative manner
    B. accept the resistance on the part of the client
    C. ignore the client's resistance
    D. recognize that little more will be accomplished in the interview and suggest another appointment

18.____

19. *Most* definitions of interviewing would NOT include the following as a necessary aspect:

    A. The interviewer and client meet face-to-face and talk things out
    B. The client is experiencing considerable emotional disturbance
    C. A valuable learning opportunity is provided for the client
    D. The interviewer brings a special competence to the relationship

19.____

20. A powerful dynamic in the interviewing process and often the very *antonym* of its counterpart in the instructional process is

    A. encouraging accuracy
    B. emphasizing structure
    C. pointing up sequential and orderly thinking
    D. processing ambiguity and equivocation

20.____

21. Interviewing techniques are frequently useful in working with clients. A basic fundamental is an atmosphere which may BEST be described as

    A. non-threatening
    B. motivating for creativity
    C. highly charged to stimulate excitement
    D. fairly-well structured

21.____

22. In interviewing the disadvantaged client, the subtle technique of steering away from high-level educational and vocational plans must be *replaced* by

    A. a wait-and-see explanation to the client
    B. the use of prediction tables to determine possibilities and probabilities of overcoming this condition
    C. avoidance in discussing controversial issues of deprivation
    D. encouragement and concrete consideration for planning his future

22.____

23. The process of collecting, analyzing, synthesizing and interpreting information about the client should be

    A. completed prior to interviewing
    B. completed early in the interviewing process
    C. limited to a type of interviewing which is primarily diagnostic in purpose
    D. continuously pursued throughout interviewing

23.____

24. Catharsis, the "emotional unloading" of the client's feelings, has a value in the early stages of interviewing because it accomplishes all BUT which one of the following goals? It

   A. relieves strong physiological tensions in the client
   B. increases the client's axiety and aggrandizes his motivation to continue counseling
   C. provides a strong substitute for "acting out" the client's aggressive feelings
   D. releases emotional energy which the client has been using to bulwark his defenses

24.____

25. In the interviewing process, the interviewer should *usually* give information

   A. whenever it is needed
   B. at the end of the process
   C. in the introductory interview
   D. just before the client would ordinarily request it

25.____

KEY (CORRECT ANSWERS)

1.	B	11.	C
2.	D	12.	D
3.	A	13.	D
4.	B	14.	D
5.	C	15.	C
6.	B	16.	D
7.	C	17.	B
8.	D	18.	B
9.	A	19.	B
10.	D	20.	D

21.	A
22.	D
23.	D
24.	B
25.	A

TEST 2

DIRECTIONS: Each question or incomplete statement is followed by several suggested answers or completions. Select the one that BEST answers the question or completes the statement. *PRINT THE LETTER OF THE CORRECT ANSWER IN THE SPACE AT THE RIGHT.*

1. Of the following problems that might affect the conduct and outcome of an interview, the MOST troublesome and *usually* the MOST difficult for the interviewer to control is the

    A. tendency of the interviewee to anticipate the needs and preferences of the interviewer
    B. impulse to cut the interviewee off when he seems to have reached the end of an idea
    C. tendency of interviewee attitudes to bias the results
    D. tendency of the interviewer to do most of the talking

1.____

2. The supervisor *most likely* to be a good interviewer is one who

    A. is adept at manipulating people and circumstances toward his objective
    B. is able to put himself in the position of the interviewee
    C. gets the more difficult questions out of the way at the beginning of the interview
    D. develops one style and technique that can be used in any type of interview

2.____

3. A good interviewer guards against the tendency to form an overall opinion about an interviewee on the basis of a single aspect of the interviewee's makeup.
This statement refers to a well-known source of error in interviewing known as the

    A. assumption error   B. expectancy error
    C. extension effect   D. halo effect

3.____

4. In conducting an "exit interview" with an employee who is leaving voluntarily, the interview's MAIN objective should be to

    A. see that the employee leaves with a good opinion of the organization
    B. learn the true reasons for the employee's resignation
    C. find out if the employee would consider a transfer
    D. try to get the employee to remain on the job

4.____

5. During an interview, an interviewee unexpectedly discloses a relevant but embarrassing personal fact.
It would be BEST for the interviewer to

    A. listen calmly, avoiding any gesture or facial expression that would suggest approval or disapproval of what is related
    B. change the subject, since further discussion in this area may reveal other embarrassing, but irrelevant, personal facts
    C. apologize to the interviewee for having led him to reveal such a fact and promise not to do so again
    D. bring the interview to a close as quickly as possible in order to avoid a discussion which may be distressing to the interviewee

5.____

6. Suppose that, while you are interviewing an applicant for a position in your office, you notice a contradiction in facts in two of his responses.
For you to call the contradictions to his attention would be

    A. *inadvisable,* because it reduces the interviewee's level of participation
    B. *advisable,* because getting the facts is essential to a successful interview
    C. *inadvisable,* because the interviewer should use more subtle techniques to resolve any discrepancies
    D. *advisable,* because the interviewee should be impressed with the necessity for giving consistent answers

6.____

7. An interviewer should be aware that an *undesirable* result of including "leading questions" in an interview is to

    A. cause the interviewee to give "yes" or "no" answers with qualification or explanation
    B. encourage the interviewee to discuss irrelevant topics
    C. encourage the interviewee to give more meaningful information
    D. reduce the validity of the information obtained from the interviewee

7.____

8. The kind of interview which is *particularly* helpful in getting an employee to tell about his complaints and grievances is one in which

    A. a pattern has been worked out involving a sequence of exact questions to be asked
    B. the interviewee is expected to support his statements with specific evidence
    C. the interviewee is not made to answer specific questions but is encouraged to talk freely
    D. the interviewer has specific items on which he wishes to get or give information

8.____

9. Suppose you are scheduled to interview an employee under your supervision concerning a health problem. You know that some of the questions you will be asking him will seem embarrassing to him, and that he may resist answering these questions.
In general, to hold these questions for the *last* part of the interview would be

    A. *desirable;* the intervening time period gives the interviewer an opportunity to plan how to ask these sensitive questions
    B. *undesirable;* the employee will probably feel that he has been tricked when he suddenly must answer embarrassing questions
    C. *desirable;* the employee will probably have increased confidence in the interviewer and be more willing to answer these questions
    D. *undesirable;* questions that are important should not be deferred until the end of the interview

9.____

10. In conducting an interview, the BEST types of questions with which to begin the interview are those which the person interviewed is

    A. willing and able to answer
    B. willing but unable to answer
    C. able to but unwilling to answer
    D. unable and unwilling to answer

10.____

11. In order to determine accurately a child's age, it is BEST for an interviewer to rely on   11.____

    A. the child's grade in school   B. what the mother says
    C. birth records   D. a library card

12. In his first interview with a new employee, it would be LEAST appropriate for a unit super-   12.____
visor to

    A. find out the employee's preference for the several types of jobs to which he is able
to assign him
    B. determine whether the employee will make good promotion material
    C. inform the employee of what his basic job responsibilities will be
    D. inquire about the employee's education and previous employment

13. If an interviewer takes care to phrase his questions carefully and precisely, the result will   13.____
most probably be that

    A. he will be able to determine whether the person interviewed is being truthful
    B. the free flow of the interview will be lost
    C. he will get the information he wants
    D. he will ask stereotyped questions and narrow the scope of the interview

14. When, during an interview, is the person interviewed LEAST likely to be cautious about   14.____
what he tells the interviewer?

    A. Shortly after the beginning when the questions normally suggest pleasant associa-
tions to the person interviewed
    B. As long as the interviewer keeps his questions to the point
    C. At the point where the person interviewed gains a clear insight into the area being
discussed
    D. When the interview appears formally ended and goodbyes are being said

15. In an interview held for the purpose of getting information from the person interviewed, it   15.____
is sometimes desirable for the interviewer to repeat the answer he has received to a
question.
For the interviewer to rephrase such an answer in his *own* words is good practice
MAINLY because it

    A. gives the interviewer time to make up his next question
    B. gives the person interviewed a chance to correct any possible misunderstanding
    C. gives the person interviewed the feeling that the interviewer considers his answer
important
    D. prevents the person interviewed from changing his answer

16. There are several methods of formulating questions during an interview. The particular   16.____
method used should be adapted to the interview problems presented by the person
being questioned.
Of the following methods of formulating questions during an interview, the *acceptable*
one is for the interviewer to ask questions which

    A. incorporate several items in order to allow a cooperative interviewee freedom to
organize his statements
    B. are ambiguous in order to foil a distrustful interviewee

C. suggest the correct answer in order to assist an interviewee who appears confused
D. would help an otherwise unresponsive interviewee to become more responsive

17. For an interviewer to permit the person being interviewed to read the data the interviewer writes as he records the person's responses on a routine departmental form, is   17.____

A. *desirable*, because it serves to assure the person interviewed that his responses are being recorded accurately
B. *undesirable*, because it prevents the interviewer from clarifying uncertain points by asking additional questions
C. *desirable*, because it makes the time that the person interviewed must wait while the answer is written seem shorter
D. *undesirable*, because it destroys the confidentiality of the interview

18. Of the following methods of conducting an interview, the BEST is to   18.____

A. ask questions with "yes" or "no" answers
B. listen carefully and ask only questions that are pertinent
C. fire questions at the interviewee so that he must answer sincerely and briefly
D. read standardized questions to the person being interviewed

---

KEY (CORRECT ANSWERS)

1.	A	11.	C
2.	B	12.	B
3.	D	13.	C
4.	B	14.	D
5.	A	15.	B
6.	B	16.	D
7.	D	17.	A
8.	C	18.	B
9.	C		
10.	A		

INTERPRETING STATISTICAL DATA
GRAPHS, CHARTS AND TABLES
TEST 1

DIRECTIONS : Study the following graphs,charts,and/or tables. Base your answers to the questions that follow SOLELY on the information contained therein. *PRINT THE LETTER OF THE CORRECT ANSWER IN THE SPACE AT THE RIGHT.*

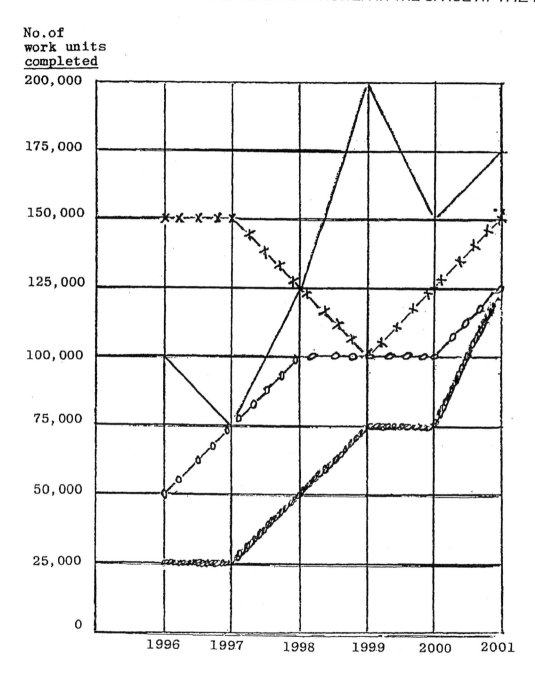

No.of
work units
completed

Units of each type of work completed by a public agency from 1996 to 2001.

```
Letters Written    _____
Documents Filed    —X——X——X——X
Applications Processed ——0——0——0——0
Inspections Made  oooooomoomoooooooooo
```

1. The year for which the number of units of one type of work completed was *less* than it was for the previous year while the number of each of the other types of work completed was *more* than it was for the previous year was

    A. 1997   B. 1998   C. 1999   D. 2000

  1.____

2. The number of letters written EXCEEDED the number of applications processed by the *same* amount in

    A. two of the years   B. three of the years
    C. four of the years   D. five of the years

  2.____

3. The YEAR in which the number of each type of work completed was *greater* than in the preceding year was

    A. 1998   B. 1999   C. 2000   D. 2001

  3.____

4. The number of applications processed and the number of documents filed were the SAME in

    A. 1997   B. 1998   C. 1999   D. 2000

  4.____

5. The *total number* of units of work completed by the agency

    A. increased in each year after 1996
    B. decreased from the prior year in two of the years after 1996
    C. was the same in two successive years from 1996 to 2001
    D. was less in 1996 than in any of the following years

  5.____

6. For the year in which the number of letters written was twice as high as it was in 1996, the number of documents FILED was

    A. the same as it was in 1996
    B. two-thirds of what it was in 1996
    C. five-sixths of what it was in 1996
    D. one and one-half times what it was in 1996

  6.____

7. The *variable* which was the MOST stable during the period 1996 through 2001 was

    A. Inspections Made   B. Letters Written
    C. Documents Filed   D. Applications Processed

  7.____

KEY (CORRECT ANSWERS)

1.	B	5.	C
2.	B	6.	B
3.	D	7.	D
4.	C		

TEST 2

Questions 1-8.

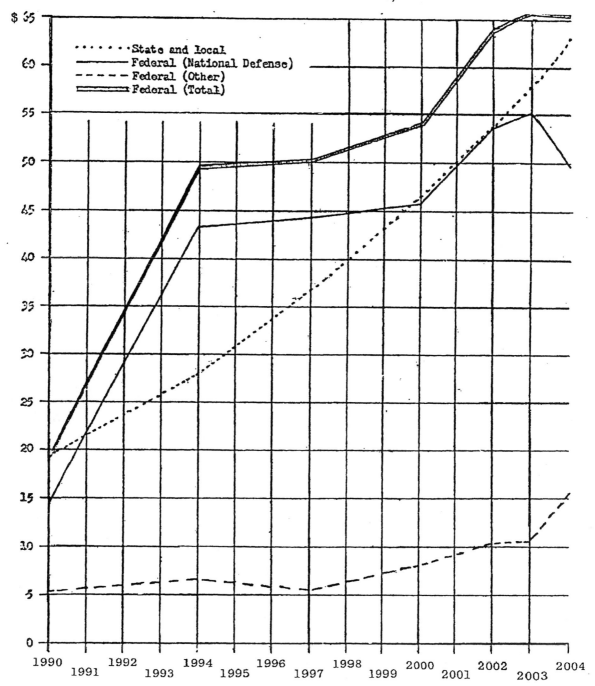

GOVERNMENT PURCHASES OF GOODS AND SERVICE
(IN BILLIONS OF DOLLARS)

Legend:
- · · · · · State and local
- ——— Federal (National Defense)
- – – – Federal (Other)
- ═════ Federal (Total)

1. Purchases by the Federal government for non-defense purposes, and purchases by State and local governments comprised the smallest proportion of the total government purchases of goods and services for all purposes in which of the following years?

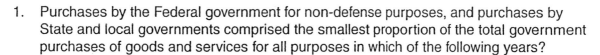

    A. 1990   B. 1994   C. 1997   D. 2000

1.____

2. Which one of the following MOST closely approximates the percentage increase in State and local purchases of goods and services in 2004 as compared with 1990? 2._____

    A. 110%   B. 150%   C. 220%   D. 350%

3. Total government purchases of goods and services in 2004 was MOST NEARLY, billion dollars. 3._____

    A. 80   B. 110   C. 128   D. 144

4. In 2000, purchases made by State and local governments 4._____

    A. exceeded Federal government total purchases
    B. exceeded purchases made by them in 1994 by more than 50%
    C. increased less than 10% over 1997
    D. were less than 50% of purchases made by them in 2003

5. Purchases of goods and services for national defense in 1994 by the Federal government was, *MOST NEARLY,* 5._____

    A. 15%less than the total spent by Federal, State and local governments for all purposes in 1990
    B. 50% of the total spent by Federal, State and local governments for all purposes in 1997
    C. four times the amount spent in 1990 for national defense
    D. ten times the amount spent in 1994 by the Federal government for purposes other than national defense

6. In which one of the following years did State and local purchases of goods and services comprise the GREATEST proportion of the total spent by all government jurisdictions? 6._____

    A. 1990   B. 1994   C. 1997   D. 2002

7. The dollar increase in purchases of goods and services was LEAST for which one of the following? 7._____

    A. State and local governments between 1990 and 1994
    B. State and local governments between 1997 and 2000
    C. Total Federal government between 2000 and 2002
    D. Federal government other than national defense between 2000 and 2003

8. The rate of increase in Federal purchases of goods and services for national defense was GREATEST between which of the following periods? 8._____

    A. From 1994 to 1997   B. From 1997 to 2000
    C. From 2000 to 2002   D. From 2002 to 2004

KEY (CORRECT ANSWERS)

1.	B	5.	B
2.	C	6.	A
3.	C	7.	D
4.	B	8.	C

TEST 3

Questions 1-10.

DIRECTIONS: Questions 1-10 are to be answered SOLELY on the basis of the following table showing the amounts purchased by various purchasing units during 2000.

DOLLAR VOLUME PURCHASED BY EACH PURCHASING UNIT DURING EACH QUARTER OF 2000
(Figures Shown Represent Thousands of Dollars)

Purchasing Unit	First Quarter	Second Quarter	Third Quarter	Fourth Quarter
A	578	924	698	312
B	1,426	1,972	1,586	1,704
c	366	494	430	716
D	1,238	1,708	1,884	1,546
E	730	742	818	774
F	948	1,118	1,256	788

1.   The TOTAL dollar volume purchased by *all* of the purchasing units during 2000 approximated, *most nearly,*

   A. $2,000,000   B. $4,000,000   C. $20,000,000   D. $40,000,000

1.____

2.   During which quarter was the GREATEST total dollar amount of purchases made?

   A. First   B. Second   C. Third   D. Fourth

2.____

3.   Assume that the dollar volume purchased by Unit F during 2000 exceeded the dollar volume purchased by Unit F during 1999 was 50%. Then the dollar volume purchased by Unit F during 1999 was

   A. $2,055,000   B. $2,550,000   C. $2,740,000   D. $6,165,000

3.____

4.   Which *one* of the following purchasing units showed the SHARPEST decrease in the amount purchased during the *fourth* quarter as compared with the *third* quarter? Unit

   A. A   B. B   C. D   D. E

4.____

5.   Comparing the dollar volume purchased in the *second* quarter with the dollar volume purchased in the *third* quarter, the *decrease* in the dollar volume during the third quarter was PRIMARILY due to the decrease in the dollar volume purchased by Units

   A. A and B   B. C and D   C. C and E   D. C and F

5.____

6.   Of the following, the unit which had the LARGEST number of dollars of increased purchases from any one quarter to the next following quarter was Unit

   A. A   B. B   C. C   D. D

6.____

7.   Of the following, the unit with the LARGEST dollar volume of purchases during the *second half* of 2000 was Unit

   A. A   B. B   C. D   D. F

7.____

8. Which one of the following *most closely* approximates the percentage which Unit B's total 2000 purchases represents of the total 2000 purchases of all units, including Unit B?   8.____

    A. 10%   B. 15%   C. 25%   D. 45%

9. Assume that research showed that each ten thousand dollars ($10,000) of purchases by Unit D during 2000 required an average of thirteen (13) man-hours of buyers' staff time. On that basis, which *one* of the following *most closely* approximates the NUMBER OF MAN-HOURS of buyers' staff time required by Unit D during 2000? _____ man-hours.   9.____

    A. 1,800   B. 8,000   C. 68,000   D. 78,000

10. Assume that research showed that each ten thousand dollars ($10,000) of purchases by Unit C during 2000 required an average of ten (10) man-hours of buyers' staff time. This research also showed that during 2000 the average man-hours of buyers' staff time per ten thousand dollars of purchases required by Unit C exceeded by 25% the average man-hours of buyers' staff time per ten thousand dollars of purchases required by Unit E. On that basis, which *one* of the following *most closely* approximates the NUMBER OF BUYER'S STAFF MAN-HOURS required by Unit E during 2000? _____ man-hours   10.____

    A. 2,200   B. 2,400   C. 3,000   D. 3,700

KEY (CORRECT ANSWERS)

1.	C	6.	B
2.	B	7.	C
3.	C	8.	C
4.	A	9.	B
5.	A	10.	B

TEST 4

Questions 1-6.

DIRECTIONS: Questions 1 to 6 are to be answered SOLELY on the basis of the following table and graph and the accompanying notes.

CONSUMER PROTECTION DIVISION-METROPOLITAN CITY
Number and Kinds of Violations (2002-2004)

NATURE OF VIOLATION	2002						2003						2004					
	District						District						District					
	A	B	C	D	E	Total	A	B	c	D	E	Total	A	B	C	D	E	Total
Scales	27	31	42	16	12	128	18	34	36	15	19	122	20	28	31	12	10	101
Gasoline sales	12	9	17	6	3	47	9	4	19			32	6	5	16	3	6	36
Illegal meat coloring	9	8	13	4		34	10	12	21	9	2	54	8	6	5	2	1	22
Fat content-chopped meat	21	19	40	7	1	88	20	17	31	3	3	74	16	12	18	4	3	53
Checkout counter errors	12	9	10	2		33	12	8	21			41	16	21	9	2	2	50
Fuel oil sales	6	5	4		16	31			2		6	8	5	6	6		18	35
Fraudulent labels	18	29	39	14	14	114	21	36	31	12	18	118	12	25	19	15	25	96
TOTALS	105	110	165	49	46	475	90	111	161	39	48	449	83	103	104	38	65	393

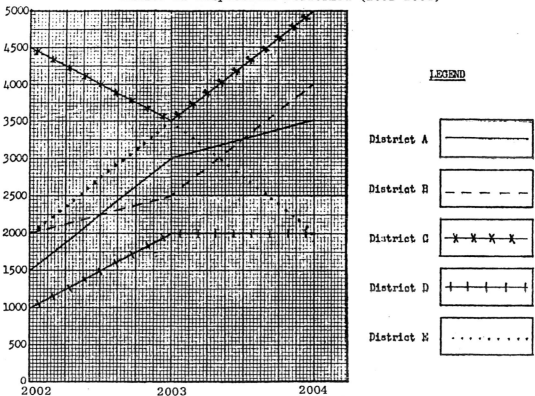

CONSUMER PROTECTION DIVISION-METROPOLITAN CITY
Number of Inspections Performed (2002-2004)

LEGEND

District A ————
District B — — —
District C ✗✗✗✗
District D ╂╂╂╂
District E ·········

NOTES: The Consumer Protection Division of Metropolitan City is divided into five districts designated A, B, C, D and E.

Number of establishments in each district:

District A - 26,000	District C - 27,000	District E - 12,000
District B - 30,000	District D - 15,000	

Number of field inspectors assigned to each district in 2002 and 2003

District A - 20	District C - 25	District # - 11
District B - 24	District D - 21	

At the beginning of 2004 there was a general reassignment of field inspectors and the staff of field inspectors was increased. This resulted in assignments of field inspectors as follows:

District A - 20	District C - 32	District E - 16
District B - 26	District D - 16	

1. Of the following districts, the one in which the ratio of meat coloring violations to total number of violations in the district was GREATEST in 2003 is District

   A. A   B. B   C. C   D. D

2. In 2003, the number of violations uncovered per field inspector for the entire city was, *most nearly*,

   A. 3.9   B. 4.1   C. 4.4   D. 4.8

3. In 2002, the number of violations per 1,000 establishments in District C was, *most nearly*,

   A. 3.9   B. 6.1   C. 10.4   D. 16.5

4. The number of inspections performed by the Consumer Protection Division in 2003 was, most *nearly*,

   A. 449   B. 12,000   C. 13,500   D. 14,500

5. In 2002, the number of violations uncovered per 100 inspections for the entire city was, *most nearly*,

   A. .23   B. 3.2   C. 4.3   D. 48.0

6. If it had been decided at the beginning of 2004 to assign inspectors so that the ratio of the number of inspectors in each district to the total number of inspectors would be the same as the ratio of the number of establishments in the district to the total number of establishments in the city, the number of inspectors assigned to District A would have been

   A. 24   B. 25   C. 26   D. 27

KEY (CORRECT ANSWERS)

1. D
2. C
3. B
4. D
5. C
6. C

TEST 5

Questions 1-4.

DIRECTIONS: Questions 1 to 4 are to be answered SOLELY on the basis of the following
graph and the accompanying notes.(Graph appears on the following page.)

NOTES: The graph shows space allocation in three municipal food markets in a certain
city. The five columns for each market represent the total amount of each market's space. The miscellaneous column accounts for all non-rental space allocated to shopping aisles, loading facilities,etc.

Assume that during 2004 there was no tenant turnover and that the amount of space
rented and unrented remained constant.
The rental charges in 2004 for all types of business were as follows:
Jefferson Market - $10.00 per square foot
Jackson Market - $17.50 per square foot
Lincoln Market - $15.00 per square foot

2004 SPACE ALLOCATIONS IN THE JEFFERSON,JACKSON AND LINCOLN MUNICIPAL
FOOD MARKETS
(According to Type of Business)

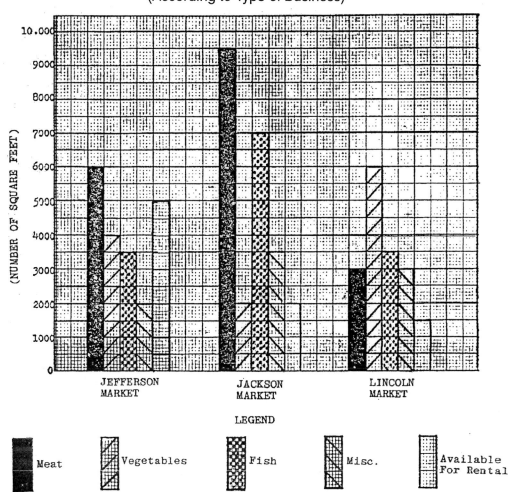

1. The percentage of over-all space in the Lincoln Market leased to fish dealers in 2004 is, *most nearly,*   1._____

    A. 17%   B. 19%   C. 21%   D. 23%

2. The total amount of space in all three municipal food markets devoted to the *meat business* EXCEEDED the amount of space in these markets devoted to the *fish business* by _____ square feet.   2._____

    A. 2,500   B. 4,500   C. 14,000   D. 18,500

3. If all of the space in the Lincoln Market available for rental in 2004 had been rented, the income received from this market would have INCREASED by   3._____

    A. 6%   B. 12%   C. 18%   D. 24%

4. Approximately what percent of the 2004 rental income of the Jackson Market was derived from vegetable dealers?   4._____

    A. 8.3%
    B. 9.1%
    C. 10.8%
    D. a percent which cannot be determined from the data given

---

KEY (CORRECT ANSWERS)

1. C
2. B
3. B
4. C

TEST 6

Questions 1-5.

DIRECTIONS: Questions 1 to 5 involve calculation of annual grade averages for college students who have just completed their junior year. These averages are to be based on the following table showing the number of credit hours for each student during the year at each of the grade levels: A,B,C,D,and F. How these letter grades may be translated into numerical grades is indicated in the first column of the table.

Grade Value	Credit hours - Junior Year					
	King	Lewis	Mart in	Norris	Ott	Perry
A = 95	12	12	9	15	6	3
B = 85	9	12	9	12	18	6
C = 75	6	6	9	3	3	21
D = 65	3	3	3	3	-	-
F = 0	-	-	3	-	-	-

NOTES: Calculating a grade average for an individual student is a 4-step process:
  I.   Multiply each grade value by the number of credit hours for which the student received that grade.
  II. Add these multiplication products for each student.
  III. Add the student's total credit hours.
  IV. Divide the multiplication product total by the total number of credit hours.
  V.   Round the result, if there is a decimal place, to the nearest whole number. A number ending in .5 would be rounded to the next higher number.

EXAMPLE: Using student King's grades as an example, his grade average can be calculated by going through the following four steps:

```
I.        95   x 12  =   1140      III.      12
          85   x  9  =    765                9
          75   x  6  =    450                6
          65   x  3  =    195                3
           0   x  0  =      0                0
II.       TOTAL  =    2550                  30   TOTAL credit hours
                                  IV.   Divide 2550 by 30: 2550 / 30 = 85
```

King's grade average is 85.
Now answer questions 1 through 5 on the basis of the information given above.

1. The grade average of Lewis is

   A. 83   B. 84   C. 85   D. 86

2. The grade average of Martin is

   A. 72   B. 73   C. 74   D. 75

3. The grade average of Norris is

   A. 85   B. 86   C. 87   D. 88

1.____

2.____

3.____

4. Student Ott must attain a grade average of 90 in each of his years in college to be accepted into the graduate school of his choice. If, in summer school during his junior year, he takes two 3-credit courses and receives a grade of 95 in each one, his grade average for his junior year will then be, *most nearly*.

    A. 87   B. 88   C. 89   D. 90

4._____

5. If Perry takes an additional 3-credit course during the year and receives a grade of 95, his grade average will be increased to *approximately*

    A. 79   B. 80   C. 81   D. 82

5._____

KEY (CORRECT ANSWERS)

1. C
2. D
3. C
4. B
5. B

TEST 7

Questions 1-5.

DIRECTIONS: Questions 1 to 5 are to be answered SOLELY on the basis of the chart below which relates to the increase in taxes.

Increase In State and Local Taxes Per Person

	1987	1999	Percent Increase		1987	1999	Percent Increase
Delaware	$138	$372	170	Iowa	$180	9389	116
Maryland	161	411	156	Tennessee	118	252	114
New York	227	576	153	Arkansas	103	221	114
Nebraska	144	362	151	Wyoming	193	414	114
Kentucky	111	278	150	New Mexico	151	324	114
Rhode bland	153	379	148	Idaho	156	328	110
Virginia	128	314	145	Pennsylvania	162	340	109
Arizona	163	387	13S	South Dakota	169	353	108
Indiana	141	334	137	Illinois	179	373	108
New Jersey	173	406	135	South Carolina	108	225	108
Wisconsin	187	439	135	Maine	149	308	106
California	232	540	133	Ohio.	149	306	105
Michigan	184	428	132	Colorado	189	386	104
Missouri	132	301	128	Nevada	232	466	101
North Carolina	115	259	125	Connecticut	196	392	100
Vermont	173	384	123	Kansas	173	346	100
Minnesota	183	406	122	Texas	139	276	99
West Virginia	119	263	120	Utah	166	327	98
Massachusetts	206	453	119	New Hampshire	152	299	97
Alabama	103	224	118	North Dakota	176	338	92
Washington	189	410	117	Oregon	204	387	90
Florida	153	330	116	Oklahoma	152	287	89
Georgia	125	270	116	Louisiana	160	298	86
Mississippi	112	242	116	Montana	189	351	86

1. The dollar increase per person in taxes between 1987-1999 was GREATEST in which state?   1._____

    A. New York   B. California   C. Wisconsin
    D. New Jersey   E. Delaware

2. The state whose people paid the LOWEST amount per person in taxes in 1999 was   2._____

    A. Montana   B. Mississippi   C. Alabama
    D. Arkansas   E. South Carolina

3. Which of the following states DOUBLED its taxes from 1987 to 1999?   3.____

    A. Kentucky   B. North Carolina   C. Kansas
    D. Texas   E. None of these

4. Which state had the SMALLEST $ increase in taxes from 1987 to 1999?   4.____

    A. Montana   B. Alabama   C. Arkansas
    D. Mississippi   E. South Carolina

5. In which of the following states was the per capita tax the GREATEST in 1987?   5.____

    A. Massachusetts   B. New York   C. Nevada
    D. Delaware   E. Oregon

KEY (CORRECT ANSWERS)

1. A
2. D
3. C
4. E
5. C

TEST 8

Questions 1-6.

DIRECTIONS: Questions 1 to 6 are to be answered SOLELY on the basis of the chart below which relates to the Distribution of Minority Groups by Pay Category.

TABLE 1-- DISTRIBUTION OF ALL MINORITY GROUPS COMBINED, BY PAY CATEGORY AS OF NOVEMBER 30, 1999 AND MAY 31, 2000

Pay System	November 1999		May 2000		Percent Change
	Number	Percent	Number	Percent	
All Pay Systems	500,508	100.0	501,871	100.0	0.3
General Schedule and Similar	181,725	36.3	186,170	37.1	2.4
Wage Systems	155,744	31.1	151,919	30.3	-2.5
Postal Field Service	158,945	31.8	159,211	31.7	0.2
All Other	4,094	0.8	4,571	0.9	11.7

1. From the table, what was the TOTAL of government workers in *all* pay systems in November, 1999?

   A. 155,744   B. 181,725   C. 186,170
   D. 500,508   E. None of these

2. What was the percentage difference between Wage Systems and All Pay Systems in November,1999, and Postal Field Service and All Pay Systems in May, 2000?

   A. .2%   B. .6%   C. 1.1%   D. 1.7%   E. 2.5%

3. How many more minority group members were employed by the Postal Field Service in May,2000 than in November,1999?

   A. .2%   B. 256   C. 266   D. 1256   E. 1266

4. In which of the pay systems did the percentage of minority workers decline?

   A. General Schedule and Similar   B. Wage Systems
   C. Postal Field Service   D. All Other
   E. None of these

5. In which system was the percentage gain of minority members from 1999 to 2000 the greatest?

   A. General Schedule and similar   B. Wage Systems
   C. Postal Field Service   D. All Other systems
   E. One cannot tell from the information given

6. Which system reflects the GREATEST percentage increase from 1999 to 2000 to the total minority work force?

   A. General Schedule and similar   B. Wage systems
   C. Postal Field Service   D. All Other
   E. One cannot tell from the information given

KEY (CORRECT ANSWERS)

1. E
2. B
3. C
4. B
5. D
6. A

———

GLOSSARY OF PERSONNEL TERMS

CONTENTS

GLOSSARY OF PERSONNEL TERMS

A

Abandonment of Position—When an employee quits work without resigning. (715)

Absence Without Leave (AWOL) Absence — without prior approval, therefore without pay, that may be subject to disciplinary action. See also, *Leave Without Pay,* which is an approved absence. (630)

Administrative Workweek— A period of seven consecutive calendar days designated in advance by the head of the agency. Usually an administrative workweek coincides with a calendar week. (610)

Admonishment— Informal reproval of an employee by a supervisor; usually oral, but some agencies require written notice. (751)

Adverse Action— A removal, suspension, furlough without pay for 30 days or less, or reduction-in-grade or pay. An adverse action may be taken against an employee for disciplinary or non-disciplinary reasons. However, if the employee is covered by FPM part 752, the action must be in accordance with those procedures. Removals or reductions-in-grade based solely on unacceptable performance are covered by Part 432. Actions taken for reductions-in-force reasons are covered by Part 351. (752)

Affirmative Action — A policy followed closely by the Federal civil service that requires agencies to take positive steps to insure equal opportunity in employment, development, advancement, and treatment of all employees and applicants for employment regardless of race, color, sex, religion, national origin, or physical or mental handicap. Affirmative action also requires that specific actions be directed at the special problems and unique concerns in assuring equal employment opportunity for minorities, women and other disadvantaged groups.

Agreement—See *Collective Bargaining.*

Annuitant—A retired Federal civil service employee or a survivor (spouse or children) being paid an annuity from the Retirement Fund. (831)

Annuity—Payments to a former employee who retired, or to the surviving spouse or children. It is computed as an annual rate but paid monthly. (831)

Appeal—A request by an employee for review of an agency action by an outside agency: The right to such review-is provided by law or regulation and may include an adversary-type hearing and a written decision in which a finding of facts is made and applicable law, Executive order and regulations are applied.

Appointing Officer—A person having power by law or lawfully delegated authority to make appointments. (210, 311)

Appointment, Noncompetitive— Employment without competing with others, in the sense that it is done without regard to civil service registers, etc. Includes reinstatements, transfers, reassignments, demotions, and promotion. (335)

Appointment, Superior Qualifications—Appointment of a candidate to a position in grade 11 or above of the General Schedule at a rate above the minimum because of the candidate's superior qualifications. A rate above the minimum for the grade must be justified by the applicant's unusually high or unique qualifications, a special need of the Government for the candidate's services, or because the candidate's current pay is higher than the minimum for the grade which he or she is offered. (338, 531)

Appointment, TAPER—Abbreviation for "temporary appointment pending establishment of a register." Employment made under an OPM authority granted to an agency when there are insufficient eligibles on a register appropriate to fill the position involved. (316)

Appointment, Temporary Limited—Nonpermanent appointment of an employee hired for a specified time of one year or less, or for seasonal or intermittent positions. (316)

Appointment, Term—Nonpermanent appointment of an employee hired to work on a project expected to last over one year, but less than four years. (316)

Appropriate Unit—A group of employees which a labor organization seeks to represent for the purpose of negotiating agreements; an aggregation of employees which has a clear and identifiable community of interest and which promotes effective dealings and efficiency of operations. It may be established on a plant or installation, craft, functional or other basis. (Also known as bargaining unit, appropriate bargaining unit.) (711)

Arbitration—Final step of the negotiated grievance procedure which may be invoked by the agency or the union (not the employee) if the grievance has not been resolved. Involves use of an impartial arbitrator selected by the agency and union to render a binding award to resolve the grievance. (711)

Arbitrator—An impartial third party to whom disputing parties submit their differences for decision (award). An *ad hoc* arbitrator is one selected to act in a specific case or a limited group of cases. A permanent arbitrator is one selected to serve for the life of the agreement or a stipulated term, hearing all disputes that arise during this period. (711)

Area Office (OPM)—Forcal point for administering and implementing all OPM programs, except investigations, in the geographic area assigned. Provides personnel management advice and assistance to agencies, and personnel evaluation, recruiting and examining and special program leadership. Principal source of employment information for agencies and the public.

Audit, Work—Visit to an employee or his supervisor to verify or gather information about a position. Sometimes called "desk audit."

B

Bargaining Rights—Legally recognized right of the labor organization to represent employees in negotiations with employers. (711)

Bargaining Unit—An appropriate grouping of employees represented on an exclusive basis by a labor organization. "Appropriate" for this purpose means that it is a grouping of employees who share a community of interest and which promotes effective union and agency dealings and efficient agency operations. (711)

Basic Workweek—For a full-time employee, the 40-hour non overtime work schedule within an administrative workweek. The usual workweek consists of five 8-hour days, Monday through Friday. (610)

Break in Service—The time between separation and reemployment that may cause a loss of rights or privileges. For transfer purposes, it means not being on an agency payroll for one working day or more. For the three-year career conditional period or for reinstatement purposes, it means not being on an agency payroll for over 30 calendar days. (315)

Bumping—During reduction-in-force, the displacement of one employee by another employee in a higher group or subgroup. (351)

C

Career—Tenure of a permanent employee in the competitive service who has completed three years of substantially continuous creditable Federal service. (315)

Career-Conditional—Tenure of a permanent employee in the competitive service who *has not* completed three years of substantially continuous creditable Federal service. (315)

Career Counseling—Service available to employees to assist them in: (1) assessing their skills, abilities, interests, and aptitudes; (2) determining qualifications required for occupations within the career system and how the requirements relate to their individual capabilities; (3) defining their career goals and developing plans for reaching the goals; (4) identifying and assessing education and training opportunities and enrollment procedures; (5) identifying factors which may impair career development; and (6) learning about resources, inside or outside the agency, where additional help is available. (250)

Career Development—Systematic development designed to increase an employee's potential for advancement and career change. It may include classroom training, reading, work experience, etc. (410)

Career Ladder—A career ladder is a series of developmental positions of increasing difficulty in the same line of work, through which an employee may progress to a journeyman level on his or her personal development and performance in that series.

Career Reserved Position—A position within SES that has a specific requirement for impartiality. May be filled" only by career appointment. (920)

Ceiling, Personnel—The maximum number of employees authorized at a given time. (312)

Certification—The process by which eligibles are ranked, according to regulations, for appointment or promotion consideration. (332, 335)

Certification, Selective—Certifying only the names of eligibles who have special qualifications required to fill particular vacant positions. (332)

Certification, Top of the Register—Certifying in regular order, beginning with the eligibles at the top of the register. (332)

Change in Duty Station—A personnel action that changes an employee from one geographical location to another in the same agency. (296)

Change to Lower Grade—Downgrading a position or reducing an employee's grade. See *Demotion.* (296)

Class of Positions—All positions sufficiently similar in: (1) kind or subject matter of work; (2) level of difficulty and responsibility; and (3) qualification requirements, so as to warrant similar treatment in personnel and pay administration. For example, all Grade GS-3 Clerk-Typist positions. (511)

Classified Service—See *Competitive Service* (212)

Collective Bargaining—Performance of the mutual obligation of the employer and the exclusive (employee) representative to meet at reasonable times, to confer and negotiate in good faith, and to execute a written agreement with respect to conditions of employment, except that by any such obligation neither party shall be compelled to agree to proposals, or be required to make concessions. (Also known as collective negotiations, negotiations, and negotiation of agreement.) (711)

Collective Bargaining Agreement—A written agreement between management and a labor-organization which is usually for a definite term, and usually defines conditions of employment, and includes grievance and arbitration procedures. The terms "collective bargaining agreement" and "contract" are synonymous. (711)

Collective Bargaining Unit—A group of employees recognized as appropriate for representation by a labor organization for collective bargaining. (See *Appropriate Unit*) (711)

Compensatory Time Off—Time off (hour-for-hour) granted an employee in lieu of overtime pay. (550)

Competitive Area—For reduction-in-force, that part of an agency within which employees are in competition for retention. Generally, it is that part of an agency covered by a single appointing office. (351)

Competitive Service—Federal positions normally filled through open competitive examination (hence the term "competitive service") under civil service rules and regulations. About 86 percent of all Federal positions are in the competitive service. (212)

Competitive Status—Basic eligibility of a person to be selected to fill a position in the competitive service without open competitive examination. Competitive status may be acquired by career-conditional or career appointment through open competitive examination, or may be granted by statute, executive order, or civil service rules without competitive examination. A person with competitive status may be promoted, transferred, reassigned, reinstated, or demoted subject to the conditions prescribed by civil service rules and regulations. (212)

Consultant—An advisor to an officer or instrumentality of the Government, as distinguished from an officer or employee who carries out the agency's duties and responsibilities. (304)

Consultation—The obligation of an agency to consult the labor organization on particular personnel issues. The process of consultation lies between notification to the labor organization, which may amount simply to providing information, and negotiation, which implies agreement on the part of the labor organization. (711)

Conversion—The process of changing a person's tenure from one type of appointment to another (e.g., conversion from temporary to career-conditional). (315)

D

Demotion—A change of an employee, while serving continuously with the same agency:
(a) To a lower grade when both the old and the new positions are in the General Schedule or under the same type graded wage schedule; or
(b) To a position with a lower rate of pay when both the old and the new positions are under the same type ungraded wage schedule, or are in different pay method categories. (335, 752)

Detail—A temporary assignment of an employee to different duties or to a different position for a specified time, with the employee returning to his/her regular duties at the end of the detail. (300)

Differentials—Recruiting incentives in the form of compensation adjustments justified by: (1) extraordinarily difficult living conditions; (2) excessive physical hardship; or (3) notably unhealthful conditions. (591)

Disciplinary Action—Action taken to correct the conduct of an employee; may range from an admonishment through reprimand, suspension, reduction in grade or pay, to removal from the service. (751, 752)

Displaced Employee Program—(DEP)— A system to help find jobs for career and career-conditional employees displaced either through reduction-in-force or by an inability to accept assignment to another commuting area. (330)

Downgrading—Change of a position to a lower grade. (511, 532)

Dual Compensation—When an employee receives compensation for more than one Federal position if he/she worked more than 40 hours during the week. The term is also used in connection with compensation from a full-time Federal position as well as a retirement annuity for prior military service. (550)

Duty Station—The specific geographical area in which an employee is permanently assigned. (296)

E

Eligible—Any applicant for appointment or promotion who meets the minimum qualification requirements. (337)

Employee Development—A term which may include *career development* and *upward mobility*. It may be oriented toward development for better performance on an employee's current job, for learning a new policy or procedure, or for enhancing an employee's potential for advancement. (410, 412)

Employee, Exempt—An employee exempt from the overtime provisions of the Fair Labor Standards Act. (551)

Employee, Nonexempt—An employee subject to the overtime provision of the Fair Labor Standards Act. (551)

Employee Organization— See *Labor Organization.*

Employee Relations—The personnel function which centers upon the relationship between the supervisor and individual employees. (711)

Entrance Level Position—A position in an occupation at the beginning level grade. (511)

Environmental Differential—Additional pay authorized for a duty involving unusually severe hazards or working conditions. (532, 550)

Equal Employment Opportunity—Federal policy to provide equal employment opportunity for all; to prohibit discrimination on the grounds of age, race, color, religion, sex, national origin, or physical or mental handicap; and to promote the full realization of employees' potential through a continuing affirmative action program in each executive department and agency. (713)

Equal Employment Opportunity Commission—Regulates and enforces the Federal program for insuring equal employment opportunity, and oversees the development and implementation of Federal agencies' affirmative action programs.

Equal Pay for Substantially Equal Work—An underlying principle that provides the same pay level for work at the same level of difficulty and responsibility. (271)

Examination, Assembled—An examination which includes as one of its parts a written or performance test for which applicants are required to assemble at appointed times and places. (337)

Examination— A means of measuring, in a practical and suitable manner, qualifications of applicants for employment in specific positions. (337)

Examination, Fitness-For-Duty—An agency directed examination given by a Federal medical officer or an employee-designated, agency-approved physician to determine the employee's physical, mental, or emotional ability to perform assigned duties safely and efficiently. (339, 831)

Examination, Unassembled—An examination in which applicants are rated on their education, experience, and other qualifications as shown in the formal application and any supportive evidence that may be required, without assembling for a written or performance test. (337)

Excepted Service—Positions in the Federal civil service not subject to the appointment requirements of the competitive service. Exceptions to the normal, competitive requirements are authorized by law, executive order, or regulation. (213, 302)

Exclusive Recognition—The status conferred on a labor organization which receives a majority of votes cast in a representation election, entitling it to act for and negotiate agreements covering all employees included in an appropriate bargaining unit. The labor organization enjoying this status is known as the exclusive representative, exclusive bargaining representative, bargaining agent, or exclusive bargaining agent. (711)

Executive Inventory—An OPM computerized file which contains background information on all members of the Senior Executive Service and persons in positions at GS-16 through GS-18 or the equivalent, and individuals at lower grades who have been certified as meeting the managerial criteria for SES. It is used as an aid to agencies in executive recruiting and as a planning and management tool. (920)

Executive Resources Board—Panel of top agency executives responsible under the law for conducting the merit staffing process for career appointment to Senior Executive Service (SES) positions in the agency. Most Boards are also responsible for setting policy on and overseeing such areas as SES position planning and executive development. (920)

F

Federal Labor Relations Authority (FLRA)—Administers the Federal service labor-management relations program. It resolves questions of union representation of employees; prosecutes and adjudicates allegations of unfair labor practices; decides questions of what is or is not negotiable; and on appeal, reviews decisions of arbitrators. (5 USC 7104)

Federal Personnel Manual (FPM)—**The** official publication containing Federal personnel regulations and guidance. Also contains the code of Federal civil service law, selected Executive orders pertaining to Federal employment, and civil service rules. (171)

Federal Service Impasses Panel (FSIP)—Administrative body created to resolve bargaining impasses in the Federal service. The Panel may recommend procedures, including arbitration, for settling impasses, or may settle the impasse itself. Considered the legal alternative to strike in the Federal sector. (711)

Federal Wage System (FWS)—A body of laws and regulations governing the administrative processes related to trades and laboring occupations in the Federal service. (532)

Full Field Investigation—Personal investigation of an applicant's background to determine whether he/she meets fitness standards for a critical-sensitive Federal position. (736)

Function—All, or a clearly identifiable segment, of an agency's mission, including all the parts of the mission (e.g. procurement), regardless of how performed. (351)

G

General Position—A position within the Senior Executive Service that may be filled by a career, noncareer, or limited appointment. (920)

General Schedule—(GS)The graded pay system as presented by Chapter 51 of Title 5, United States Code, for classifying positions. **(511)**

Grade—All classes of positions which, although different with respect to kind or subject matter of work, are sufficiently equivalent as to (1) level of difficulty and responsibility, and (2) level of qualification requirements of the work to warrant the inclusion of such classes of positions within one range of rates of basic compensation. (511, 532)

Grade Retention—The right of a General Schedule or prevailing rate employee, when demoted for certain reasons, to retain the higher grade for most purposes for two years. (536)

Grievance, (Negotiated Procedure)—Any complaint or expressed dissatisfaction by an employee against an action by management in connection with his job, pay or other aspects of employment. Whether such complaint or expressed dissatisfaction is formally recognized and handled as a "grievance" under a negotiated procedure depends on the scope of that procedure. (711)

Grievance (Under Agency Administrative Procedure)—A request by an employee or by a group of employees acting as individuals, for personal relief in a matter of concern or dissatisfaction to the employee, subject to the control of agency management.

Grievance Procedure—A procedure, either administrative or negotiated, by which employees may seek redress of any matter subject to the control of agency management. (711, 771)

H

Handbook X-118— The official qualification standard a manual for General Schedule Positions. (338)

Handbook X-118C—The official qualification standards manual for Wage System positions. (338)

Hearing—The opportunity for contending parties under a grievance, complaint, or other remedial process, to introduce testimony and evidence and to confront and examine or cross examine witnesses. (713, 771, 772)

I

Impasse Procedures—Procedures for resolving deadlocks between agencies and union in collective bargaining. (711)

Incentive Awards—An all-inclusive term covering awards granted under Part 451 or OPM regulations. Includes an award for a suggestion submitted by an employee and adopted by management; a special achievement award for performance exceeding job requirements, or an honorary award in the form of a certificate, emblem, pin or other item. (451)

Indefinite—Tenure of a nonpermanent employee hired for an unlimited time. (316)

Injury, Work Related—For compensation under the Federal Employees' Compensation Act, a personal injury sustained while in the performance of duty. The term "injury" includes diseases proximately caused by the employment. (810)

Injury, Traumatic—Under the Federal Employees' Compensation Act, for continuation of pay purposes, a wound or other condition of the body caused by external force, including stress or strain. The injury must be identifiable by time and place of occurrence and member or function of the body affected, and be caused by a specific event or incident or series of events or incidents within a single day or work shift. (810)

Intergovernmental Personnel Assignment—Assignments of personnel to and from the Executive Branch of the Federal Government, state and local government agencies, and institutions of higher education up to two years, although a two-year extension may be permitted. The purpose is to provide technical assistance or expertise where needed for short periods of time. (334)

Intermittent—Less than full-time employment requiring irregular work hours which cannot be prescheduled. (610)

J

Job Analysis—Technical review and evaluation of a position's duties, responsibilities, and level of work and of the skills, abilities, and knowledge needed to do the work. (511, 532)

Job Enrichment—Carefully planned work assignments and/or training to use and upgrade employee skills, abilities, and interests; and to provide opportunity for growth, and encourage self-improvement. (312)

Job Freeze—A restriction on hiring and/or promotion by administrative or legislative action. (330)

Job Title— The formal name of a position as determined by official classification standards. (511, 532)

Journeyman Level—(Full Performance Level)The lowest level of a career ladder position at which an employee has learned the full range of duties in a specific occupation. All jobs below full performance level are developmental levels, through which each employee in the occupation may progress to full performance. (511)

L

Labor-Management Relations—Relationships and dealings between employee unions and management. (711)

Labor Organization—An organization composed in whole or in part of employees, in which employees participate and pay dues, and which has as a purpose dealing with an agency concerning grievances and working conditions of employment. (711)

Lead Agency—Under the Federal Wage-System, the Federal agency with the largest number of Federal wage workers in a geographical area; consequently, it has the primary role for determining wage rates for all Federal employees who work in that area and are covered by the System. (532)

Leave, Annual—Time allowed to employees for vacation and other absences for personal reasons. (630)

Leave, Court—Time allowed to employees for jury and certain types of witness service. (630)

Leave, Military—Time allowed to employees for certain types of military service. (630)

Leave, Sick—Time allowed to employees for physical incapacity, to prevent the spread of contagious diseases, or to obtain medical, dental or eye examination or treatment. (630)

Leave Without Pay (LWOP)—A temporary nonpay status and absence from duty, requested by an employee. The permissive nature of "leave without pay" distinguishes it from "absence without leave." (630)

Level of Difficulty—A classification term used to indicate the relative ranking of duties and responsibilities. (511, 532)

M

Maintenance Review—A formal, periodic review (usually annual) of all positions in an organization, or portion of an organization, to insure that classifications are correct and position descriptions are current. (511)

Major Duty—Any duty or responsibility, or group of closely related tasks, of a position which (1) determines qualification requirements for the position, (2) occupies a significant amount of the employee's time, and (3) is a regular or recurring duty. (511)

Management Official—An individual employed by an agency in a position whose duties and responsibilities require or authorize the individual to formulate, determine or influence the policies of the agency. (711)

Management Rights—The right of management to make day-today personnel decisions and to direct the work force without mandatory negotiation with the exclusive representative. (See "Reserved Rights Doctrine.") Usually a specific list of management authorities not subject to the obligation to bargain. (117)

Mediation—Procedure using a third-party to facilitate the reaching of an agreement voluntarily. (711)

Merit Promotion Program—The system under which agencies consider an employee for internal personnel actions on the basis of personal merit. (335)

Merit Systems Protection Board (MSPB)—An independent agency which monitors the administration of the Federal civil service system, prosecutes and adjudicates allegations of merit principle abuses, and hears and decides other civil service appeals. (5 USC 1205)

N

National Agency Check and Inquiry (NACI)—The Investigation of applicants for nonsensitive Federal positions by means of a name check through national investigative files and voucher inquiries. (731)

National Consultation Rights—A relationship established between the headquarters of a Federal agency and the national office of a union under criteria of the Federal Labor Relations Authority. When a union holds national consultation rights, the agency must give the union notice of proposed new substantive personnel policies, and of proposed changes in personnel policies, and an opportunity to comment on such proposals. The union has a right to: (1) suggest changes in personnel policies and have those suggestions carefully considered; (2) consult at reasonable times with appropriate officials about personnel policy matters; and (3) submit its views in writing on personnel policy matters at any time. The agency must provide the union with a written statement (which need not be detailed) of reasons for taking its final action on a policy. (711)

Negotiability—A determination as to whether a matter is within the obligation to bargain. (711)

Negotiated Grievance Procedure—A procedure applicable to members of a bargaining unit for considering grievances. Coverage and scope are negotiated by the parties to the agreement, except that the procedures may not cover certain matters designated in Title VII of the CSRA as excluded from the scope of negotiated grievance procedures. (711)

Negotiations—The bargaining process used to reach a settlement between labor and management over conditions of employment. (711)

Nominating Officer—A subordinate officer of an agency to whom authority has been delegated by the head of the agency to nominate for appointment but not actually appoint employees. (311)

O

Objection—A written statement by an agency of the reasons why it believes an eligible whose name is on a certificate is not qualified for the position to which referred. If the Examining Office sustains the objection, the agency may eliminate the person from consideration. (332)

Occupational Group—Positions of differing kinds but within the same field of work. For example, the GS-500 Accounting and Budget Occupational Group includes: General Accounting Clerical and Administrative Series; Financial Management; Internal Revenue Agent Accounting Technician; Payroll; etc. (511, 532)

Office of Personnel Management (OPM)—Regulates, administers, and evaluates the civil service program according to merit principles. (5 USC 1103)

Office of Workers Compensation Programs (OWCP)—In the Department of Labor, administers statutes that allow compensation to employees and their survivors for work-related injuries and illnesses. Decides and pays claims. (810)

Official Personnel Folder (OPF)—The official repository of employment records and documents affecting personnel actions during an employee's Federal civilian service. (293)

Overtime Work—Under Title 5, U.S. Code, officially ordered or approved work performed in excess of eight hours in a day or 40 hours in a week. Under the Fair Labor Standards Act, work in excess of 40 hours in a week by a nonexempt employee. (550, 551)

P

Pass Over—Elimination from appointment consideration of a veteran preference eligible on a certificate (candidate list), to appoint a lower ranking nonveteran, when the agency submits reasons which OPM finds sufficient. (332)

Pay Retention—The right of a General Schedule or prevailing rate employee (following a grade retention period or at other specified times when the rate of basic pay would otherwise be reduced) to continue to receive the higher rate. Pay is retained indefinitely. (536)

Pay, Severance—Money paid to employees separated by reduction-in-force and not eligible for retirement. The following formula is used, but the amount cannot be more than one year's pay:
   Basic Severance Pay— One week's pay for each year of civilian service up to 10 years, and two weeks' pay for each year served over 10 years, plus
   Age Adjustment Allowance —10 percent of the basic severance pay for each year over age 40. (550)

Performance Appraisal—The comparison, under a performance appraisal system, of an employee's actual performance against the performance standards previously established for the position. (430)

Personal Action— The process necessary to appoint, separate, reinstate, or make other changes affecting an employee (e.g., change in position assignment, tenure, etc.). (296)

Personnel Management—Management of human resources to accomplish a mission and provide individual job satisfaction. It is the line responsibility of the operating supervisor and the staff responsibility of the personnel office. (250)

Position—A specific job consisting of all the current major duties and responsibilities assigned or delegated by management. (312)

Position Change—A promotion, demotion, or reassignment. (335)

Position Classification—Analyzing and categorizing jobs by occupational group, series, class, and grade according to like duties, responsibilities, and qualification requirements. (511, 532)

Position Classifier—A specialist in job analysis who determines the titles, occupational groups, series, and grades of positions. (312)

Position Description—An official written statement of the major duties, responsibilities and supervisory relationships of a position. (312)

Position Management—The process of designing positions to combine logical and consistent duties and responsibilities into an orderly, efficient, and productive organization to accomplish agency mission. (312)

Position Survey—Agency review of positions to determine whether the positions are still needed and, if so, whether the classification and position description are correct. (312)

Position, "PL 313 Type"—Positions established under Public Law 80-313 of August 1, 1947, or similar authorities. A small group of high level professional and scientific positions generally in the competitive service, but not filled through competitive examinations. Salaries are set between GS-12 and GS-18. (534)

Preference, Compensable Disability ("CP")—Ten-point preference awarded to a veteran separated under honorable conditions from active duty, who receives compensation of 10 percent or more for a service-connected disability. Eligible "CP" veterans are placed at the top of civil service lists of eligibles for positions at GS-9 or higher. (211)

Preference, 30 Percent or More, Disabled ("CPS")—A disabled veteran whose disability is rated at 30 percent or more, entitled to special preference in appointment and during reduction in force.

Preference, Disability ("XP")—Ten-point preference in hiring for a veteran separated under honorable conditions from active duty and who has a service-connected disability or receives compensation, pension, or disability retirement from the VA or a uniformed service. (211)

Preference, Mother ("XP")—Ten-point preference to which the mother of a deceased or disabled military veteran may be entitled. (211)

Preference, Spouse ("XP")—Ten-point preference to which a disabled military veteran's spouse may be entitled. (211)

Preference, Tentative ("TP")— Five-point veteran preference tentatively awarded an eligible who served on active duty during specified periods and was separated from military service under honorable conditions. It must be verified by the appointing officer. (211)

Preference, Veteran—The statutory right to special advantage in appointments or separations; based on a person's discharge under honorable conditions from the armed forces, for a service-connected disability. *Not* applicable to the Senior Executive Service. (211)

Preference, Widow or Widower ("XP")—Ten-point preference to which a military veteran's widow or widower may be entitled. (211)

Premium Pay—Additional pay for overtime, night, Sunday and holiday work. (550)

Prevailing Rate System—A subsystem of the Federal Wage System used to determine the employee's pay in a particular wage area. The determination requires, comparing. the_. rate of pay with the private sector for similar duties and responsibilities. (532)

Probationary Period—A trial period which is a condition of the initial competitive appointment. Provides the final indispensable test of ability, that of actual performance on the job. (315)

Promotion—A change of an employee to a higher grade when both the old and new positions are under the same job classification system and pay schedule, or to a position with higher pay in a different job classification system and pay schedule. (335)

Promotion, Career—Promotion of an employee without current competition when: (1) he/ she had earlier been competitively selected from a register or under competitive promotion procedures for an assignment intended as a matter of record to be preparation for the position being filled; or (2) the position is reconstituted at a higher grade because of additional duties and responsibilities. (335)

Promotion, Competitive—Selection of a current or former Federal civil service employee for a higher grade position, using procedures that compare the candidates on merit. (335)

Promotion Certificate—A list of best qualified candidates to be considered to fill a position under competitive promotion procedures. (335)

Q

Qualifications Review Board—A panel attached to OPM that determines whether a candidate for career appointment in the Senior Executive Service meets the managerial criteria established by law.

Qualification Requirements—Education, experience, and other prerequisites to employment or placement in a position. (338)

Quality Graduate—College graduate who was a superior student and can be hired at a higher grade than the one to which he/she would otherwise be entitled '(338)

Quality Increase—An additional within-grade increase granted to General Schedule employees for high quality performance above that ordinarily found in the type of position concerned (531).

R

Reassignment—The change of an employee, while serving continuously within the same agency, from one position to another, without promotion or demotion. (210)

Recognition—Employer acceptance of a labor organization as authorized to negotiate, usually for all members of a bargaining unit. (711) Also, used to refer to incentive awards granted under provisions of Parts 451 and 541 of OPM Regulations, and Quality Increases granted under Part 531.

Recruitment—Process of attracting a supply of qualified eligibles for employment consideration. (332)

Reduction-in-Force (RIF)—A personnel action that may be required due to lack of work or funds, changes resulting from reorganization, downward reclassification of a position, or the need to make room for an employee with reemployment or restoration rights. Involves separating an employee from his/her present position, but does not necessarily result in separation or downgrading. (351) (See also *Tenure Groups.*)

Reemployment Priority List—Career and career-conditional employees, separated by reduction-in-force, who are identified, in priority order, for reemployment to competitive positions in the agency in the commuting area where the separations occurred. (330)

Reemployment Rights—Right of an employee to return to an agency after detail, transfer, or appointment to: (1) another Executive agency during an emergency; (2) an international organization; or (3) other statutorily covered employment, e.g., the Peace Corps. (352)

Register—A list of eligible applicants compiled in the order of their relative standing for referral to Federal jobs, after competitive civil service examination. (332,210)

Reinstatement— Noncompetitive reemployment in the competitive service based on previous service under a career or career-conditional appointment. (315)

Removal—Separation of an employee for cause or because of continual unacceptable performance. (432, 752)

Representation—Actions and rights of the labor organization to consult and negotiate with management on behalf of the bargaining unit and represent employees in the unit. (711)

Representation Election—Election conducted to determine whether the employees in an appropriate unit (See *Bargaining Unit*) desire a labor organization to act as their exclusive representative. (711)

Reprimand—An official rebuke of an employee. Normally in writing and placed in the temporary side of an employee's OPF-(751)

"Reserved Rights Doctrine"—Specific functions delegated to management by Title VII of CSRA that protect management's ability to perform its necessary functions and duties. (See Management Rights.) Delegates to management specific functions not subject to negotiation except as to procedures and impact. (711)

Resignation—A separation, prior to retirement, in response to an employee's request for the action. It is a voluntary expression of the employee's desire to leave the organization and must not be demanded as an alternative to some other action to be taken or withheld. (715)

Restoration Rights—Employees who enter military service or sustain a compensable job-related injury or disability are entitled to be restored to the same or higher employment status held prior to their absence. (353)

Retention Preference—The relative standing of employees competing in a reduction-inforce. Their standing is determined by veteran's preference, tenure group, length of service, and performance appraisal. (351)

Retention Register—A list of all employees, arranged by competitive level, describing their retention preference during reductions-in-force. (351)

Retirement—Payment of an annuity after separation from a position under the Civil Service Retirement System and based on meeting age and length of service requirements. The types of retirement are:

> *Deferred* - An employee with five years civilian service who separates or transfers to a position not under the Retirement Act, may receive an annuity, does not withdraw from the Retirement Fund. (.83:1)
> *Disability* - An immediate annuity paid to an employee under the retirement system who has completed five years of civilian service and has suffered a mental, emotional, or physical disability not the result of the employee's vicious habits, intemperance, or willful misconduct, (831)
> *Discontinued Service* - An immediate annuity paid to an employee who is involuntarily sepa-rated, through no personal fault of the employee, after age 50 and 20 years of service, or at any age with 25 years of service. This annuity is reduced by 1/6 of one percent for each full month under age 55 (two percent per year). (831)
> *Optional* - The minimum combinations of age and service for this kind of immediate annuity are: age 62 with five years of service; age 60 with 20 years of service; age 55 with 30 years of service. (831)

Review, Classification—An official written request for reclassification of a position. Previously called a classification appeal.

S

Schedules A, B, and C—Categories of positions excepted from the competitive service by regulation. (213)

> *Schedule A—Positions* other than confidential or policy determining, for which it is not practical to examine.
>
> *Schedule B*— Positions other than confidential or policy determining for which it is not practical to hold a competitive examination.
>
> *Schedule C*—Positions of a confidential or policy determining character.

Senior Executive Service—A separate personnel system for persons who set policy and administer programs at the top levels of the Government (equivalent to GS-16 through Executive Level IV). (920)

Service Computation Date-Leave—The date, either actual or adjusted, from which service credit is accumulated for determining the rate of leave accrual; it may be different from the service computation date, which determines relative standing in a subgroup for reduction-in-force, or service computation date for retirement. (296)

Service Record Card (Standard Form 7)—A brief of the employee's service history. It is kept on file in accordance with agency disposition instructions. (295)

Special Salary Rates—Salary rates higher than regular statutory schedule; established for occupations in which private enterprise pays substantially more than the regular Federal Schedule. (530)

Spoils System—The personnel system characterized by the political appointment and removal of employees without regard to merit. (212)

Staffing—Use of available and projected personnel through recruitment, appointment, reassignment, promotion, reduction-in-force, etc., to provide the work force required to fulfill the agency's mission. (250)

Standard Form—171 ("Personal Qualification Statement") Used in applying for a Federal position through a competitive examination. (295)

Standards of Conduct For Labor Organization—In the Federal sector, a code governing internal democratic practices and fiscal responsibility, and procedures to which a labor organization must adhere to be eligible to receive any recognition. (711)

Steward (Union Steward)—A local union's representative in a plant or department, appointed by the union to carry out union duties, adjust grievances, collect dues and solicit new members. Stewards are employees trained by the union to carry out their duties.

Strike—Temporary stoppage of work by a group of employees to express a grievance, enforce a demand for changes in conditions of employment, obtain recognition, or resolve a dispute with management. *Wildcat strike-* a strike not sanctioned by union and which may violate a collective agreement. *Quickie strike-* a spontaneous or unannounced strike of short duration. *Slowdown-a* deliberate reduction of output without an actual strike in order to force concessions from *an* employer. *Walkout -*same as strike. Strikes are illegal for Federal employees. (711)

Suitability—An applicant's or employee's fitness for Federal employment as indicated by character and conduct. (731)

Supervisor—An individual employed by an agency having authority, in the interest of the agency, to hire, direct, assign, promote, reward, transfer, furlough, lay off, recall, suspend, discipline-or remove employees, to adjust their grievances, or to effectively recommend such action-if the exercise of the authority is not merely routine or clerical in nature but requires the consistent exercise of independent judgment. With respect to any unit which includes firefighters or nurses, the term "supervisor" includes only those individuals who devote a preponderance of their employment time to exercising such authority. (711).

Survey, Classification—An intensive study of all positions in an organization or organizational segment to insure their correct classification.

Suspension—Placing an employee, for disciplinary reasons, in a temporary status without duties and pay. (751, 752)

T

Tenure—The time an employee may reasonably expect to serve under a current appointment. It is governed by the type of appointment, without regard to whether the employee has competitive status. (210)

Tenure Groups—Categories of employees ranked in priority order for retention during reduction in force . Within each group, veterans are ranked above nonveterans. For the competitive service, the tenure groups are, in descending order:
    Group I—Employees under career appointments and not serving probation.
    Group II—Employees serving probation, career-conditional employees, and career employees in obligated positions.
    Group III—Employees with indefinite appointments, status quo employees under any other nonstatus, nontemporary appointment. (351)
For the *excepted service,* they are in descending order:
    Group I—Permanent employees, not serving a trial period, whose appointments carry no restriction or condition, such as "indefinite" or "time-limited".
    Group II—Employees serving trial periods, those whose tenure is indefinite because they occupy obligated positions, and those whose tenure is equivalent to career-conditional in the competitive service.
    Group III—Employees whose tenure is indefinite, but not potentially permanent, and temporary employees who have completed one year of current continuous employment. (351)

Tenure Subgroups—The ranking of veterans above nonveterans in each tenure group, as follows:

Subgroup AD—Veterans with service-connected disability of 30% or more.
Subgroup A— All other veterans
Subgroup B—Nonveterans

Time-in-Grade Restriction—A requirement intended to prevent excessively rapid promotions in the General Schedule. Generally, an employee may not be promoted more than two grades within one year to positions up to GS-5. At GS-5 and above, an employee must serve a minimum of one year in grade, and cannot be promoted more than one grade, or two grades if that is the normal progression. (300)

Tour of Duty—The hours of a day (a daily tour of duty) and the day of an administrative workweek (weekly tour of duty) scheduled in advance and during which an employee is required to work regularly. (610)

Training—Formal instruction or controlled and planned exposure to learning. (410)

Transfer—A change of an employee, without a break in service of one full workday, from a position in one agency to a position in another agency. (315)

Transfer of Function—For reduction-in-force, the transfer of a continuing function from one agency or competitive area to another, or when the competitive area in which work is performed is moved to another commuting area. (315)

U

Unemployment Compensation—Income maintenance payments to former Federal employees who: (1) are unemployed; (2) file a claim at a local employment office for unemployment compensation; and (3) register for work assignment. The program is administered through state and D.C. employment service offices, which determine eligibility and make the payments. (850)

Unfair Labor Practices—Prohibited actions by agency management and labor organizations. (711)

Union—See *Labor Organization.*

Upward Mobility—Systematic career development requiring competitive selection in positions that provide experience and training leading to future assignments in other, more responsible positions.(410)

V

Veteran—A person entitled to preference under 5 USC 2108, including a spouse, widow, widower, or mother entitled to preference under the law. (211)

Voucher—In staffing terms, a formal inquiry to employers, references, professors, and others who presumably know a job applicant well enough to describe job qualifications and personal character. (337)

W

Wage Employees—Those employees-in trades, crafts, or labor occupations covered by the Federal Wage System, whose pay is fixed and adjusted periodically in accordance with prevailing rates. (532)

Within-Grade Increase—A salary increase provided in certain Government pay plans based upon time-in-grade and acceptable or satisfactory work performance. Also known as "periodic increase" or "step increase." (531)

NOTE:

Numbers in parentheses after the definitions refer to the appropriate FEDERAL PERSONNEL MANUAL (FPM) Chapter indicated.

ANSWER SHEET

TEST NO. _____ PART _____ TITLE OF POSITION _____

(AS GIVEN IN EXAMINATION ANNOUNCEMENT - INCLUDE OPTION, IF ANY)

PLACE OF EXAMINATION _____ DATE ___ _____

(CITY OR TOWN)   (STATE)

RATING

USE THE SPECIAL PENCIL.   MAKE GLOSSY BLACK MARKS.

	A B C D E		A B C D E		A B C D E		A B C D E		A B C D E
1		26		51		76		101	
2		27		52		77		102	
3		28		53		78		103	
4		29		54		79		104	
5		30		55		80		105	
6		31		56		81		106	
7		32		57		82		107	
8		33		58		83		108	
9		34		59		84		109	
10		35		60		85		110	

Make only ONE mark for each answer.   Additional and stray marks may be
counted as mistakes.   In making corrections, erase errors COMPLETELY.

	A B C D E		A B C D E		A B C D E		A B C D E		A B C D E
11		36		61		86		111	
12		37		62		87		112	
13		38		63		88		113	
14		39		64		89		114	
15		40		65		90		115	
16		41		66		91		116	
17		42		67		92		117	
18		43		68		93		118	
19		44		69		94		119	
20		45		70		95		120	
21		46		71		96		121	
22		47		72		97		122	
23		48		73		98		123	
24		49		74		99		124	
25		50		75		100		125	

ANSWER SHEET

TEST NO. _____ PART _____ TITLE OF POSITION _____

PLACE OF EXAMINATION _____ DATE _____ _____

(CITY OR TOWN)   (STATE)

RATING

USE THE SPECIAL PENCIL.   MAKE GLOSSY BLACK MARKS.

	A B C D E		A B C D E		A B C D E		A B C D E		A B C D E
1		26		51		76		101	
2		27		52		77		102	
3		28		53		78		103	
4		29		54		79		104	
5		30		55		80		105	
6		31		56		81		106	
7		32		57		82		107	
8		33		58		83		108	
9		34		59		84		109	
10		35		60		85		110	

Make only ONE mark for each answer.   Additional and stray marks may be counted as mistakes.   In making corrections, erase errors COMPLETELY.

	A B C D E		A B C D E		A B C D E		A B C D E		A B C D E
11		36		61		86		111	
12		37		62		87		112	
13		38		63		88		113	
14		39		64		89		114	
15		40		65		90		115	
16		41		66		91		116	
17		42		67		92		117	
18		43		68		93		118	
19		44		69		94		119	
20		45		70		95		120	
21		46		71		96		121	
22		47		72		97		122	
23		48		73		98		123	
24		49		74		99		124	
25		50		75		100		125	